# A.W. TOZER

*Compiled and Edited by James L. Snyder*

# GOD'S POWER FOR YOUR LIFE

## HOW THE HOLY SPIRIT TRANSFORMS YOU THROUGH GOD'S WORD

**BETHANYHOUSE**

*a division of Baker Publishing Group*
Minneapolis, Minnesota

Published by Bethany House Publishers
11400 Hampshire Avenue South
Bloomington, Minnesota 55438
www.bethanyhouse.com

Bethany House Publishers is a division of
Baker Publishing Group, Grand Rapids, Michigan

Bethany House edition published 2014
ISBN 978-0-7642-1619-0

Previously published by Regal Books

Printed in the United States of America

Library of Congress Control Number: 2014955663

Scripture quotations are from the King James Version of the Bible.

15   16   17   18   19   20   21        8   7   6   5   4   3   2

# CONTENTS

# CAN WE TRUST THE BIBLE?

An important discussion among today's Christians revolves around the topic of power. This is not a new conversation. Many books have been published on the subject of spiritual power, and some are even quite helpful. Dr. Tozer was deeply concerned with this issue; specifically, he was troubled by the obvious impotence, despite all of these books on spiritual power, of the average Christian.

At the heart of the matter is this simple question: *Can we trust the Bible?* So much is being said and written about Scripture today that some have become confused about the importance of the Bible.

Throughout this book, Dr. Tozer lays down the simple truth that the Bible was never designed to replace God but to bring us radically and directly into the presence of God. The Bible is not a textbook informing us of what we should believe, nor a religious book telling us the proper way to worship. Certainly, those things are in the Scripture, but they are not the primary purpose of the Word of God.

"Get on your knees with an outspread Bible," Dr. Tozer encourages us, "and linger in the presence of God." How many of us really know what it means to come into the presence of God and linger there? The purpose of this book is to encourage believers to seek God as He desires to be sought.

Nothing in this world is permanent, save the Word of God. When we know "thus saith the Lord," we know all that needs to be known. We know what we need to know to delight ourselves in the sanctuary of divine power.

Much of the talk about power today has to do with promoting someone's individual agenda. Even some preachers want to demonstrate the awesomeness of their power and draw attention to how spiritual they are. Many speak of the miracles they have done. Now, anybody who has read the Bible believes in the authenticity of miracles—that is not the question. The question has to do with the purposes for which power is exercised.

The power associated with the Word of God and the Holy Spirit is that power that brings us into the manifest presence of God. You will encounter that phrase over and over in this book. It is a phrase unfamiliar to most Christians today, but the truth is that we must come into the presence of God. God is not an absentee God; He is not "Someone up there who likes me." The great delight of our Father in heaven is to have fellowship with the redeemed.

The whole purpose of our redemption was to bring us back into sweet and wonderful fellowship with the Father. Salvation is not just about going to heaven. Certainly, our destination is heaven, but our salvation has afforded us a relationship with God that is personal and intimate right now. How many believers really have experienced the presence of God? How many have felt His breath upon them as they drew near in awesome reverence?

To know God in this fashion is the great delight of the believer.

Many in our generation are caught up in politics and social concerns. There's nothing wrong with this, but there is something much greater: our fellowship with God. Everything we do needs to flow out of what we are. We are Christians—and that means we are in awesome fellowship with the God of creation.

God's power, when the Holy Spirit operates through the written Word, thrusts us deeper into God's presence. That is where we need to go. We cannot get there, as Dr. Tozer admonishes in this book, through education or any other kind of outward manipulation. It is the transforming power of the Holy Spirit through the Word of God that enables us to experience God in this fashion. We should not be willing to settle for anything less.

Unfortunately, many of us have been distracted by our culture. So many things compete to occupy our attention that we fail to spend significant time with God. This book can be the beginning of a journey toward—or back to—deep fellowship with Him. Because I believe this book is important, I would like to give some simple guidelines for reading it.

Often when I get a new book, I cannot put it down until I have completely read through it. I'm a little obsessive in that way. However, I do not believe that is the best way to approach this book. Go ahead and read it through at one sitting if you must—get it out of your system—but allow me to give some suggestions so you can get the most out of this book on a second reading.

The first suggestion I would give is to read only one chapter a day so you can concentrate on a small portion at a time. Speed-reading may be fine for some books, but one like this needs to be dealt with in a different fashion.

Dr. Tozer loved quoting Francis Bacon: "Some books are to be tasted, others to be swallowed, and some few to be chewed and digested." I earnestly believe that this book falls into the last category. Take your time to slowly chew and digest the truths it contains.

Begin your reading of each chapter with the opening prayer. Slowly read the prayer, and then spend some time meditating on it until it becomes your prayer. Doing so will set up a certain level of expectation for the material at hand.

Digest the truth of the chapter. Personally, I like to read with pen in hand so I can mark certain words and phrases that stand out to me. I guess I am old-fashioned that way. If you are reading this book as an e-book, you might want to find another way to make note of key points. There is something to be said for slowly going over a passage and focusing on words and phrases that at the time speak to your heart. I am not suggesting you bypass your brain, but I am suggesting that you tarry long enough for the truth to penetrate your heart.

The last thing to do is to lovingly meditate on the hymn at the end of each chapter. The chosen hymn succinctly emphasizes the truth found within the chapter. There is something about a hymn that is unlike any other form of expression. We have drifted away from this knowledge, but as you peruse this book, I urge you to pay attention to the hymns.

I am by no means suggesting that this book is on par with the Holy Scriptures. That would be blasphemy. What I am suggesting is that there is truth in Dr. Tozer's words that can dynamically change the way a person lives. This book will make accessible to the sincere reader the power to live the Christian life in such a way as to please God.

May this book open up to you avenues of delight in your daily pursuit of God.

Rev. James L. Snyder

# God's Power for Your Life

# PART I

## THE SIGNIFICANCE OF GOD'S POWER

*Thy word have I hid in mine heart,*
*that I might not sin against thee.*
PSALM 119:11

# 1

# GOD'S UNIQUE
# THING: THE BIBLE

*Father, I pray Thee, bless this effort to tell how great Thou art and
how great and beautiful Thy Word is—how winsome and how terrible.
O Lord, no man can do it, but we try. Take our little fish and bread,
break it and divide it, O Lord. For we are only a child handing Thee
a little wicker basket with a few pieces of food—not enough for all.
O Lord, break it and multiply it. Amen.*

Certain authorities in our world are false—without foundation—and we do right to reject them. With great satisfaction,
I want to point to the one true religious authority: the supreme
authority that resides in God. God Almighty exercises that
supreme authority through His Word and through His Son.
This is the focus of this book.

Both the Old Testament and the New emphatically declare
this, and it is the unanimous belief of Jews and Christians.

God possesses this supreme authority for certain reasons,
one being His eternity. You see, God was before all other authorities. I do not say that there are not other authorities; I
well know there are. God, however, was before them. Lords,
kings, emperors and potentates have certain authorities, but
their authority is late in time; it is borrowed from God and
therefore temporary. Whatever is temporary cannot be final
and supreme.

Another kind of authority is that which God has delegated: prophets, apostles, popes, bishops and religious sages. If these appointed ones were good and wise stewards of the power with which they had been entrusted, they possessed borrowed authority; but if they were bad, they usurped it. It is entirely possible to misuse this delegated authority, and many have done so throughout the centuries. Bishops say, "Don't do so-and-so," and those under their authority dare not do it. Then in the same vein are popes, apostles and prophets. I repeat, if they were good, they borrowed their authority from God; but if they were bad, they usurped it from God. Either way, it came from God, and all had to surrender it when they died. At best, their borrowed authority was temporary.

Over against the transitory, relative and tentative authority of the prophets and apostles and kings and popes and emperors and bishops and presidents and all the rest stand these awesome words: "And, Thou, Lord, in the beginning hast laid the foundation of the earth; and the heavens are the works of thine hands" (Heb. 1:10). Before the world was, God was; and when the world finally burns itself out, God will still stand as the supreme authority. If I have to prove that, then we have no foundation at all for our faith, "for he that cometh to God must believe that he is, and that he is a rewarder of them that diligently seek him" (Heb. 11:6).

The dynamics of God's supreme authority rest upon His attributes. Some of those attributes God can share with His people: love, kindness, compassion, pity, holiness and righteousness, for instance. Some, however, are so divine that God cannot share them: self-existence, sovereignty and omniscience, among others. These attributes declare God to have all the authority there is. It would be great for us Christians if we would remember that.

# The Authoritative Word of God

How does God exercise His authority? The answer will be the foundation of our Christian experience. God exercises His authority through His Word. God speaks to man and makes His will known by this vehicle.

This book is called, among other names, the Book of God, the Book of the Lord, the Good Word of God, the Holy Writings, the Law of the Lord, the Word of Christ, the Oracles of God, the Word of Life, and the Word of Truth. These are all descriptions of that Word through which God utters His authority. This Word is said to be God-breathed, indestructible and eternal.

In this Word, we have God's unique thing. This Book of the Lord—the uttered Word of God—is different from and above and transcends all others of its kind; it is uncompromising, authoritative, awesome and eternal. It is through this Word that God exercises His supreme, self-bestowed authority—for He never took His authority from men. The Lord never kneeled and had someone touch His shoulder with a sword and say, "Rise, sovereign God." Nobody can bestow sovereignty upon the sovereign God. Any temporary sovereignty a human being possesses has been bestowed by God.

It is the nature of God to express Himself; therefore, He utters Himself forth. What He utters originates in the mind of an infinite Creator and then comes into the mind of a finite creature. Some people are so ponderously intellectual that this bothers them. It does not bother me at all. I do not believe there is any uncrossable bridge when the infinite Creator determines He is going to utter forth His authoritative Word to finite man. I believe He can do it—and in this uttered Word rests His sovereign authority with the power of life and death.

I do not believe this is too strong an expression. Indeed, the Scripture declares that the gospel is the Word of Life. The day will come when every *T* will be crossed, every *I* will be dotted, and not one iota of God's mighty Word will remain unfulfilled. God never speaks forth any frivolous word or anything out of context with His character and nature.

The Song of Solomon dramatizes the way that the Word of God came to man, saying: "Thine Almighty word leaped down from heaven out of thy royal throne, as a fierce man of war into the midst of a land of destruction" (18:15). The Word comes from the royal throne—the throne that never was built because it was always there. The throne upon which sits the mighty, almighty God.

This is why I do not like to see people tinker with the Bible. This almighty Word leaped down from the royal throne, and I have to be careful because it is that unique thing. It is the will of God revealed to me. It is God uttering forth His sovereign authority through printed words that I can read on the page. However, these words are said to be lively and dynamic and creative. When God spoke it, it was done. When He commanded it, it stood forth. Creation came by His Word. For that reason, we should never think of God as getting down on His knees and working on a piece of clay like a potter. That is a beautiful image, but the fact is that God spoke, and all things came into being.

In the first chapters of Genesis, God said, "Let there be light," and there was light. God said, "Let the earth bring forth," and it brought forth. Whatever God said happened. God says, furthermore, that there will be a day when we will see every word that He has spoken come to pass. The day will come when Jesus Christ will call all the nations before Him, and He will do it by His Word that He has uttered forth.

God's Word is both our terror and our hope; it both kills and makes alive. If we engage it in faith, humility and obedience, it gives life, cleanses, feeds and defends. If we close it in unbelief or ignore it or resist it, it will accuse us before the God who gave it. It is the living Word of God, coming like a fierce man of war with great power, and you and I dare not resist it, and we dare not argue it down.

I know people who believe part of it but do not believe other parts of it. They say that if it inspires them, it is inspired; and if it does not inspire them, it is simply history and tradition. For my part, I believe this is God's unique thing—the uttered Word of the living God—and that when we get into the meaning of it and know what God is uttering forth, it has the power to kill those who resist and the power to make alive those who believe.

"Who hath believed our report? and to whom is the arm of the LORD revealed?" (Isa. 53:1). Unbelief will paralyze the arm of man; yet the arm of the Lord, far from being paralyzed, is working for the salvation of men. There is power in God's Word, and when I believe it and engage it, and it engages me, something happens: The eternal God does an eternal act in the heart of a finite man.

## A Warning and an Invitation

God's authoritative Word sounds both a warning and an invitation. Go to your Bible and hear God say, "The soul that sinneth, it shall die" (Ezek. 18:20). And, "Except a man be born again, he cannot see the kingdom of God" (John 3:3). And, "Except ye repent, ye shall all likewise perish" (Luke 13:5). And, "Not every one that saith unto me, Lord, Lord, shall enter into the kingdom of heaven; but he that doeth the will of my Father" (Matt. 7:21). And, "Them which do iniquity . . . shall [be] cast into a furnace of fire: there shall be wailing and gnashing of teeth" (Matt. 13:41-42). And, "For this ye know, that no whoremonger, nor unclean person, nor covetous man, who is an idolater, hath any inheritance in the kingdom of Christ and of God" (Eph. 5:5).

These are the awful words of God. He is speaking forth this unique thing in His authoritative utterance. Nobody dares touch that; nobody dares rise and say, "But let us explain this in the light of what Plato said." I have read Plato, but I do not care what Plato says.

When God says, "The soul that sinneth, it shall die" (Ezek. 18:20), let Plato kneel before the authoritative Word of God, this unique and awful thing. God has spoken His authority through His Word; let no pope rise and explain that in the light of what Father So-and-so said. Let Father So-and-so be still. Let everybody keep still while God Almighty speaks. "Hear, O heavens, and give ear, O earth: for the Lord hath spoken" (Isa. 1:2).

The uttered Word is also a word of invitation. Ah, the beautiful invitation of the Word of God! This is not the result of a group of religious people meeting together, having a board meeting, and deciding that they are saying it. No, no, no. God Almighty said it. He spoke it out of heaven; it leaped down as a strong man in the night and filled the earth with the sound of His voice.

This Word says, "Let him return unto the LORD, and he will have mercy upon him" (Isa. 55:7). And, "Come unto me, all ye that labour and are heavy laden, and I will give you rest" (Matt. 11:28). And, "If thou shalt confess with thy mouth the Lord Jesus, and shalt believe in thine heart that God hath raised him from the dead, thou shalt be saved" (Rom. 10:9). And, "By grace are ye saved through faith; and that not of yourselves: it is the gift of God: Not of works, lest any man should boast" (Eph. 2:8-9).

This Word declares that "if we confess our sins, he is faithful and just to forgive us our sins, and to cleanse us from all unrighteousness" (1 John 1:9). It is the one authoritative voice that needs no editing, no interrupting, and no explaining; it only needs to be released and believed.

When asked to come and give a series of 10 lectures in defense of the Bible, C. H. Spurgeon wired back, "I won't come, the Bible needs no defense. Turn it loose and like a lion it will defend itself." I, too, believe that we do not need anybody defending the Word of God. We only need to preach it.

In Luke 16, there is an awesome passage about a rich man who had died. From hell, he lifted up his eyes and saw Abraham—and the beggar, Lazarus, in Abraham's bosom. The rich man who fared sumptuously had suddenly stopped faring so sumptuously and was now in hell, begging for a drop of water for his tongue. He did not get it, but became an evangelist, saying, "Abraham, if you won't help me, please help my five brothers, for I have five brothers back home who are not believers, and if you'll send Lazarus, maybe he can save them—maybe they'll repent."

Abraham said, "They must listen to Moses and the prophets."

The rich man pleaded again, "Please, Abraham, won't you send him to my five brothers? For if somebody rises from the dead, they'll hear him."

Abraham answered, "If they will not hear the word, they will not believe, though one rose from the dead" (see Luke 16:19-31).

God has made our future, our destiny, our faith, our hope and our grief; He has done so for the entire world and all the countless centuries yet ahead. God has made it all and tied it up with this Book. This Word of God, at the discretion of the Holy Spirit, is the power in the life of a believer, and it is not to be challenged.

God is speaking authoritatively, and nobody has any right to come in and say, "I don't believe that." All right, go your way, but the Word of the living God still sounds through the world, destroying what it does not redeem. In that awful day when God shakes all that can be shaken, that living, vibrant, awesome, all-powerful, eternal Word will destroy all that is not redeemed. I, for my part, want to be on the side of the redeemed. Many times, I get down on my knees, reading the fifty-fourth chapter of Isaiah, and let the unique thing speak to my heart. I let that awful Word talk to me, and I hear that Word speaking in a voice that goes clear to the depths of my being.

Do you want to know when they can take away the kindness of God from the people that are seeking Him? Do you want to know when they can remove the covenant of God's saving grace from the man that trusts in Him? That time will never come, though the mountain moves and is no more (see Isa. 54:10). God has said that He will never remove that mercy—for the mercy of God remains eternal and steadfast forever. These are the words of God—the means by which the Holy Spirit brings us into complete compliance with the holiness of a holy God.

## My Hope Is Built
### Edward Mote (1797–1874)

---

My hope is built on nothing less
Than Jesus' blood and righteousness.
I dare not trust the sweetest frame,
But wholly trust in Jesus' Name.

When darkness seems to hide His face,
I rest on His unchanging grace.

In every high and stormy gale,
My anchor holds within the veil.

His oath, His covenant, His blood,
Support me in the whelming flood.
When all around my soul gives way,
He then is all my Hope and Stay.

When He shall come with trumpet sound,
Oh may I then in Him be found.
Dressed in His righteousness alone,
Faultless to stand before the throne.

On Christ the solid Rock I stand,
All other ground is sinking sand;
All other ground is sinking sand.

# 2

# THE CHALLENGE TO GOD'S AUTHORITY

*I have sought Thee, O Lord, and have been confused by the false authorities that have usurped authority over Thee. May my heart be rooted in Thy Word, O God, to such an extent that Thy truth is ever precious to me. In Jesus' name. Amen.*

Once we have established the fact of God's authority, we need to prepare ourselves for the insidious challenge of the enemy to that authority. This brings me to an important consideration. That is: *What authority resides in religion, and where does it lie?* Religion plays an integral part in every human experience; those who deny religion do so quite religiously, but nobody can really get away from the long arm of religion.

So I ask again: *Where is the authority of religion?* For it wields great power over men's lives. Is there somewhere a final supreme authority whom we may trust implicitly—an authority in which we may take refuge with complete assurance—and at the same time whom we are obliged to obey?

Discovering the authentic source of authority in religion is going to be crucial to how I live my life. A growing number of people live their lives as though there were no such thing as authority in religion. If they are right, nothing really changes. However, if they are wrong about this—and I assure you they are—there is a terrific consequence.

For if such an authority exists, and we spend an entire lifetime not subjecting ourselves to that authority—missing it or ignoring it or flaunting it—we will be of all men most miserable. When at last, after a lifetime of rebellion against this authority, we are finally forced to report to it, we will find ourselves in a calamity of overwhelming proportions.

You can always tell what kind of a person a man is by his views on religion. If, for example, his idea of religion is something added when convenient, that tells me something about that man. If, on the other hand, a man's religion is the center of his life, and everything else flows from that direction, this tells me something different about a man. How you view your religion is reflected in how you live your life.

Many people live as though religion were just an incidental thing—I include many Christians in this statement. Many Christians (or at least, many of those who call themselves Christian) wear their Christianity as an adjunct to their life. They refuse to be inconvenienced by any aspect of Christianity.

Ask yourself these questions: *How has your Christianity inconvenienced your life this past week? Does your Christianity hold a place of priority in your life? Or is it merely a matter of convenience?*

## What Constitutes "Authority in Religion"?

I am employing the broadest definition of religion when I say that any final authority must answer truthfully several things.

First, it must answer the question: *Where is truth found?* If it cannot do this, I need to continue looking for another source of authority.

In addition, it must answer the question: *What am I to believe?* It must provide a system comprising the minimum that is absolutely essential to believe in.

*What must I do to be saved?* That is a crucial question. Any authority in religion that does not answer this question must be abandoned as quickly as possible. If they cannot tell me how to be saved and come into a right relationship with God, it is a spurious religion.

Then there is the question of sin, which nobody really wants to deal with in any absolute way. How we define sin says a great deal about our understanding of, and commitment to, the Word of God. *How do I deal with my sins?* If my religion ignores my sin or marginalizes the effect of my sin, I need to be very careful. What is sin but rebellion against God? If my religion does not define sin that way, I need to rethink the whole issue.

*What about my soul?* What authority does my religion have in answering the question of my soul? There is nothing more important in my life than my soul. What is my soul? How does my religion affect my soul?

The questions continue: *What about death? What about judgment after death? What about heaven? What about hell?*

One of the primary purposes of religion is to answer these kinds of questions. Beyond just answering them, true religion has the authority to do what needs to be done in light of each question.

Now we could pose many other questions, but they all boil down to this: *Where do you get your authority? Do you have any proof?*

Most religions are experts at dancing around questions like this. They have an aptitude for distracting me from the real question and posing some secondary question that points me in a different direction. But authority must have a source— and there must be solid evidence and proof of that source. Otherwise, it is false authority.

## False Authorities

What are some of the areas of false authority? These false authorities need to be named for what they are, and then dealt with according to the blessed Word of God.

We will find at least five false authorities that permeate religion today—even, I may add, the area of Christianity.

The first of these is tradition. Someone once said that a tradition is anything you do more than one time. The landscape of religion is littered with traditions these days. It seems every religion—and even every generation—has its own list of traditions that must be followed. Often, the people who are carrying them on have no idea why they do so.

A tradition has a history that cannot be supported by facts. This is crucial to understand. Beliefs and practices come to be based on that tradition. There is no other reason to do something than that it has been done that way in the past.

Then we come to this question: *Which tradition do we go with? Roman? Greek? Jewish?* These traditions are quite different from one another in many respects.

Wherever you gather all of this tradition from is simply the dustbin—the attic—of religion. Generation after generation will base their beliefs and practices upon relics, not knowing any of the reasons behind the practice or belief.

Another false authority that has invaded the church, particularly the evangelical church, is the authority of numbers. It is the size of the organization that matters. The bigger the organization, the more authority and power it has. I have never been one to base the importance or validity of an organization on a count of noses.

A simple review of history will show that the masses have never been right. Look at Noah and the people of his day. Consider Sodom and Gomorrah. Throughout the Old Testament, we see the decision-making abilities of the nation of Israel. The masses wanted Saul to be their king. We all know how that worked out.

This generation of Christians needs to understand that numbers do not make anything true. You can get a vast number of people to believe something, but if it was an error before they believed it, it is still an error after they have been convinced.

Let's say one man believes that 2 times 2 equals 7. His belief does not make the statement true. It does not matter if 100 men believe it; it still is not true. Not even if 1 million people believe most emphatically that 2 times 2 equals 7 does it become true.

One thing that is hard for today's Christians to understand is that the church is not run by democratic principles. We have one rulebook, and that is the Bible. Down through the centuries, the Church has been hurt by holding on to beliefs and practices that are contrary to Scripture. If enough people believe something to be true, then it is voted on and accepted as true. This is the basis of heresy within the confines of the Church of Jesus Christ.

A third false authority is nature—or let me call it the Native Instinct. This has gained ground recently; it is the error of the humanist and the transcendentalist. Simply put, it says, "Trust the light within you." This Native Instinct has become quite popular among certain contemporary teachers, and it has made inroads into the evangelical church.

It is bad enough that we are voting on what we believe or do not believe. But then we follow that with this philosophy about the Bible: "That part of the Bible is inspired which inspires me."

"Oh yes," these teachers tell us, "the Bible is inspired—but only those parts that inspire me. The rest of the Bible we can ignore." If we run across something in the Scriptures counter to our natural inclinations, we can dismiss it by claiming that part of Scripture is not inspired, and therefore I do not have to pay attention to it.

A fourth source of false authority comes from reason or philosophy. Here is where we get bogged down in philosophical swamps. If our authority is to come from reason or philosophy, the logical question is: *Which one? Spiritism? Naturalism? Idealism? Realism? Materialism? Intuitionism? Atheism? Humanism?*

You can jumble them all together and have a rather fine mixture on your hands. I am quite sure that in each one is something admirable and good. However, it is not what is good about the philosophy but what is bad about it that concerns me. It is not the water but the poison in the water that kills.

From a young age, I have read philosophy, psychology, and many things related to this. When you come right down to it, one is just as good as another—or I might say, one is just as bad as the other. The thing that they all have in common is that they are false authorities.

## Religion as False Authority

The final false authority I wish to mention here is religion itself. This may seem a little odd, but religion has become false authority from very near the beginning. Perhaps we could even go back to the Tower of Babel, but that is just speculation on my part.

If religion is to be our authority, again I ask: *Which one?*

Will it be Eastern, Western, monotheistic or polytheistic? Which one is the correct authority when it comes to religion? Each of these religions contradicts the others, and there can be no authority where there is contradiction. If one of these religions is right, which one is it?

This has been the dilemma down through the years. By nature, man is religious and seeks to organize his religion. Throughout the centuries, numerous religions have developed and have organized people in various sections of the world.

How do these religious organizations get started, and how do they grow? It is quite evident that most of these religions, if not all of them, have experienced a great deal of growth and development. They grow in the amount of history they have and in the numbers of adherents they can claim. It is not uncommon for many of them to be in competition with one another. Some think nothing of stealing another religion's sheep, as it were. That theft is not difficult, as many people base their choice of religion on who has the most to offer—and usually what they offer is fun, entertainment, and things of that nature.

All religions start out rather small, and those that endure grow and increase in authority century after century. Those who knew the religion when it was small are long dead. Succeeding generations never knew a time when the religious organization was not well established, so they take a respectful, reverent attitude toward it. This is what gives religion its authority.

It keeps its power and increases its awesomeness through a variety of means.

One way is through custom. No one dares challenge the authority of this religion, because they have never known a day when it did not possess that authority. The custom of their religion has become a sense of security for them.

Special dress, especially for the religious leaders, is a very important factor contributing to the awesomeness of a religion. If someone simply saw the dress, knowing nothing of the religion or its customs, he would be tempted to laugh. Much of the dress religious leaders wear has long ago lost its significance. What was once the vogue of a culture is now a comical relapse into the past. However, because of its association with the perceived authority of the religion, this outmoded dress inspires great respect among the religion's followers.

Another way religion seeks to keep its power and increase its awesomeness is through pageantry, pomp, honorifics, solemnities, magic rights, and extreme pretense of great gravity. From the outside, it looks awesome and spectacular, but on the inside it is empty and all but meaningless.

Intimidation is a tool frequently used by religion to maintain its power over people. Let me be clear here: The purpose of religion is to control people, and the most effective way to control people is through intimidation. Among the biggest weapons of intimidation are the threats of purgatory, excommunication, and so forth. Nobody wants to be excommunicated, i.e., left out and separated from the rest of the people.

Religion also keeps and increases its power through economic pressures. Whoever controls the money controls the people. It is an effective ploy of religion to use economic pressure to intimidate and control people. We must be careful that we do not fall into this trap in the evangelical church.

One often-overlooked aspect is the movement toward a one-church religion. I am not prepared to define that "one church" at this point. People always get into trouble when they try to explain what they themselves do not know. I do not know what that one-church religion is going to be; I just know that given the way things are going, we are headed towards that in the not-too-distant future. Slowly, surely, the squeeze is on to bring the world under the authority of one church. This would certainly be the most efficient way of controlling people: Whoever controls the one church controls all the people belonging to it.

From a purely humanistic standpoint, one-church religion appears to solve many problems. Those who would bind us in these religious chains plead in the interest of economic efficiency, and there is logic in that argument.

They also say that as followers of Christ we must love one another and join in brotherhood. Therefore, they embrace us while they enslave us. The pressure is upon us to consolidate our religious beliefs into one convenient, worldwide religion.

I believe the time is coming when evangelical Christians will not be able to take our Christianity as casually as we do now. The time is coming when we may have to stand up and be counted for the genuine thing.

## Not Alone for Mighty Empire
### William Pierson Merrill (1867–1954)

---

Not alone for mighty empire,
stretching far over land and sea,
not alone for bounteous harvests,
lift we up our hearts to thee.
Standing in the living present,
memory and hope between,
Lord, we would with deep thanksgiving,
praise thee more for things unseen.

Not for battleships and fortress,
not for conquests of the sword,
but for conquests of the spirit
give we thanks to thee, O Lord;
for the priceless gift of freedom,
for the home, the church, the school,
for the open door to manhood,
in a land the people rule.

For the armies of the faithful,
souls that passed and left no name;
for the glory that illumines
patriot lives of deathless fame.
For our prophets and apostles,
loyal to the living Word,
for all heroes of the spirit,
give we thanks to thee, O Lord.

God of justice, save the people
from the clash of race and creed,
from the strife of class and faction,
make our nation free indeed;
keep her faith in simple manhood
strong as when her life began,
till it find its full fruition
in the brotherhood of man!

# 3

# THE RIGHTFUL PLACE OF THE LIVING WORD

*The world, O God, is in such a confused mess. I thank Thee,*
*O God, that Thou art not the author of confusion. Although the world*
*seems to be in chaos, I praise Thee that nothing has gone out of Thy*
*hand. Behind all of the chaos, the confusion and turmoil, You, the*
*eternal God, are my refuge, and underneath are Your everlasting*
*arms. I take refuge in the truth that this is your world.*
*I rest firmly in Thy sovereignty. Amen.*

Perhaps no other generation in the history of the world has encountered such confusing times. In this day of comic strips and television, when people have long ago put their minds to rest and are only occasionally disturbed—say at income tax time or when somebody gets ill—it is hard to get a hold of certain core concepts of the Bible. In fact, it is increasingly hard for many to think for any significant length of time on any subject.

Although it looks like things are out of control, behind the scenes there is a God who has not surrendered His authority. For the time being, it may appear that He has abandoned this place we call the earth. But be assured that God is in control. His sovereignty has never been compromised, and His will has never been thwarted. Whatever the Bible has established to be true can never be otherwise.

God did not create trash; the only trash in our universe is that which man has made. One thing clearly taught in the Scriptures is that everything God made in His vast universe He made with a divine purpose. Indeed, this is our Father's world—although at the present time, the dust and the filth of sin have made of it a moral and physical cesspool.

The propriety of God in this world and in the universe is hard to grasp, because the evangelical and fundamentalist church has for so long preached only the escapist element of Christianity.

Before I go any further, I need to state very emphatically that I believe in this escapist element of Christianity. Personally, I will escape a much deserved hell as a result of Christ's death on the cross and resurrection from the dead. I believe Christ is a bridge over a chasm. I believe He is a lifeboat on a stormy, destructive sea. I believe He is the great Physician to heal our souls. I believe He is all that the poets and the hymnists and the Scriptures themselves say He is—and so much more. I believe that, but if this belief is emphasized too much—particularly if is it held exclusively—we never grasp the whole meaning of what those Scriptures are talking about when they say that God made His Son, Jesus Christ, to be heir of all things.

Similarly, those who use Christianity simply for its social and ethical value obscure the propriety of God in this world. Christianity does have its social aspects: singing hymns together and maybe going on a church picnic. We get together and mingle, talk, greet each other—and hopefully talk about the Lord.

The Old Testament prophet Malachi emphasized this aspect of faith: "Then they that feared the LORD spake often one to another: and the LORD hearkened, and heard it, and a book of remembrance was written before him for them that feared the LORD, and that thought upon his name" (Mal. 3:16).

Certainly, the Lord does not despise the social aspect of Christianity—nor the ethical aspect. Both are extremely important, and both bring to our human interactions a form or standard of righteousness. However, if we place all our emphasis upon the ethical element in Christianity—that we should be good, do good, and do that which is right—and go no further, we will never understand the overarching propriety of God in this world.

An area of the church I refer to as the "fringes of evangelicalism"—where the playboys of the gospel world are so very active and vocal—will never know what we are talking about here. Christianity has become to them a way whereby they can have a lot of nice, clean fun and still go to heaven when it is all over. I am afraid the fringes are seeping deeper toward the core of today's Christianity. The popular leaders today are the playboys with a grin as broad as a barn door, and with all 32 teeth shining in their glory. They dash about the church, whipping the congregation into a frenzy of good feeling.

To understand the place of the living Word in this present world will take some very serious and prayerful thought. We must say to ourselves, *I'm going to think this through; I'm going to pray it through and get a hold of it.* Until we do that, we are frittering our lives away on the fringe and never getting to the real meat of the Christian experience.

## Understanding God's Purposes

I am often guilty of doodling, especially when I am talking on the telephone; it is an absent-minded, no purpose kind of activity. Let me put it straight here: God never doodles. Nothing God is associated with could be defined as purposeless activity.

When God sets His mind to do a thing, that action carries with it the ramifications of eternity. To understand the Word fully, we must come to an understanding of this God behind the Word.

God never engages in anything that does not have a long-range, noble, worthy purpose behind it. This concept is not well grasped by Christians today. It is hard for the average Christian, who is committed only to playing around with Christianity, to understand the hard-core purpose of God in everything He does. Because we ourselves do many things that are inconsequential and have no purpose, we naturally carry this over into our thinking about God.

When I begin to understand God, I begin to see the purpose of His ways in the universe—and, more importantly, in my world. I begin to understand things from a divine perspective. What is God's purpose? How could we bring the purpose of God down into one statement that would cover the entire territory that we are talking about?

The purpose of God is to bring together and acquaint all beings with all other beings. When that time comes, toward which the whole creation is moving, each will see its essential oneness with all. The theological liberals talk about the brotherhood of man. What they fail to understand is that, although unity is the eternal purpose of God for mankind, sin has temporarily undermined that purpose. God wants us to be one, but Satan has used—and continues to use—the weapon of sin to fight against the supreme purpose of God.

God certainly is immanent in His universe, transcendent above His universe, and infinitely separated from His universe as the Creator God. The hymn writer James Montgomery (1771-1854) addressed this in a wonderful hymn called "The Glorious Universe Around":

The glorious universe around,
The heavens with all their train,
Sun, moon, and stars, are firmly bound,
In one mysterious chain.

The earth, the ocean, and the sky,
To form one world agree,
Where all that walk, or swim, or fly,
Compose one family.

God in creation thus displays
His wisdom and His might,
While all His works with all His ways
Harmoniously unite.

In one fraternal bond of love,
One fellowship of mind,
The saints below, and saints above,
Their bliss and glory find.

The phrase "harmoniously unite" assures us that in God's universe, when sin has been purged out of it, everything will be found consummate with everything else, and there will be universal cosmic harmony. Presently, the universe is filled with disorder and the raucous, rattling sound of sin in the world. One day that will be purged, and there will be harmonious unity of all things that swim, fly, walk, crawl and compose one family. As British poet John Dryden (1631–1700) wrote in his poem "A Song for St. Cecilia's Day":

From Harmony, from heavenly Harmony
This universal Frame began:

From Harmony to Harmony
Through all the Compass of the Notes it ran,
The Diapason closing full in Man.

The fragility of creation is seen in the present discord that is all around us: weather conditions, nation rising against nation, ongoing crime on the streets of our cities, and the rise of addiction and immorality in our society. The Bible clearly teaches that God is not the author of confusion (see 1 Cor. 14:33). The disorder so prevalent today is therefore not His design, and it will one day be done away with, as God finally does away with sin and Satan.

## Each Person Is Essential

In that day—when Christ returns in triumph, and the consummation of all things is reached—we will see clearly that everything God does has a purpose, flowing in full harmony with the eternity of God. We will also see that, in the eternal plan of God, there cannot be anybody that is not essential. From time to time, we all throw ourselves down and say, "I'm no good and I'm not necessary." Then we will understand that no man is an accident or mistake. Every person is absolutely essential to the plan of God.

A great orchestra has many instruments. As listeners, we may rate them as having varying importance, but to the conductor every instrument is essential. Take the piccolo player, for example. In the course of a symphony concert, the piccolo player may have only a few notes to play. But those few notes are essential to the whole symphonic presentation. What if in the middle of the symphony, the piccolo player were to sneak out of the orchestra, thinking nobody would miss him? The conductor surely would: He is expecting that piccolo note at the right place, and the piece will not be complete without it.

Nobody is more important than the piccolo player when the conductor is calling for the piccolo.

You may think that you are just a little piccolo note and really do not amount to anything. In that day when God brings all things to light, you will discover just how important and significant you have been in God's plan. When we see things in the fullness of God's light, all thoughts of futility will go out of our minds. Moreover, all sense of futility will disappear from the universe. Everything will have its purpose and everything will be in its place.

At that time, each person will know his unique value—value that nobody else possibly could give—and understand his unique place in the purpose and plan of God. In the grand scheme of things, we all are indispensable.

## Moving Toward Completion

As things stand now, the whole universe is in a state of incompleteness. There is a sense that we too are incomplete, like a half-built cathedral. This is the condition the world is in today, and it is the reason that when one trouble is settled, two other troubles pop up to take its place. Our world is like a mother with triplets. All three of them never sleep at the same time. As soon as one goes to sleep, the other two wake up. Maybe she can get two down to sleep, but there is always one who is going to be awake.

Out in the world there is a sense of incompleteness. World War I was to be the war that ends all wars. Not long after World War I, World War II broke out in Europe—and there has been fighting around this world ever since. When one political upheaval is settled, another one begins halfway around the world. This discord emphasizes the incompleteness of our world as it is.

The eternal purpose of God is laid out before us, so vast that only God could think of it. This eternal purpose—this vast, eternal scheme of God—seems to us all mixed up. That is because, like vandals coming in on a construction job to upset things and throw things around, the devil is causing disarray while God is building His cathedral.

But keep in mind that even the devil himself cannot stay the hand of God. He cannot prevent God from completing the cathedral that is in His mind. If we are patient and trust in God Almighty and look to Jesus Christ, it will take shape one of these days under the wise hand of that great Architect and Builder. You will then see that things have been all the time moving toward the grand completion. We do not see it yet. Our understanding is faulty. At best, we are only seeing through a glass darkly. At worst, we are stone blind.

As it is now, we see and experience only segments of things. We fail to see God's hand in things; we cannot see angels, or clouds of witnesses, or spirits of just men made perfect, or the Church of the firstborn, or the general assembly. We do not see the glory that will be ours in the day when we lean on our Bridegroom's arms and are led into the presence of the Father with exceeding joy. We can see these things only by faith—and then only imperfectly. As a result, the devil is sometimes able to discourage us, saying, "You believe, all right. But look, everything's going to pot all around you." When we get a little disheartened, as we will on occasion, we need to remind ourselves that the world around us is a work in progress, and so are we.

This seemingly incomplete world of ours will one day be completed, and then all flesh will see, behold and wonder at the glory of God. He will bring all things together as an architect brings diverse building materials together to make a beautiful finished cathedral. He will bring all things together as a composer brings notes played by various instruments together to make a beautiful symphony.

On that final day, all things will be united and displayed in Jesus Christ, who, according to Scripture, is heir of all things. This world belongs to Jesus Christ. It is He, and He alone, who makes sense of everything in this world. Take Christ out of the equation and the formula falls apart. It is Jesus Christ who makes God's creation complete.

We do not see this now, because in our time, everything is out of place.

Satan, for example, is out of place. He belongs in the Lake of Fire with all the other demons. But he is walking to and fro in the earth, accusing the brethren.

Sinners are out of place as well. They belong with the devil in hell, but they are walking up and down the earth, beating their chests and thinking they are king of the world. They have no concept of their final destination. They do not fit in anywhere, because they have rejected the core of what humanity is all about: Jesus Christ. Sin has destroyed their ability to know their place in this world.

Christ is also out of place. Right now, He is sitting on the Father's throne, sharing the throne with the Father and making intercession for you and me. Christ belongs on David's throne as Ruler and King of the universe. One of these days, Christ will step out of eternity as He did once before—on His way to the cross—and will assume His rightful place on the throne of David.

Israel is out of place, scattered throughout the world. Israel belongs back in the place called Palestine in the Holy Land. Instead, the people of Israel are scattered all over the world. Little by little, we see them gravitating back to the land of Israel. One day they all will be gathered in their rightful place. The land of Canaan—promised to them by God through Abraham, Isaac and Jacob—will one day be theirs.

The Church is out of place. The Church belongs with her Bridegroom in the Father's house. At present, she is scattered all over the world—struggling, praying, laboring and suffering for the cause of Christ. The Church should be ruling the world—and one day will do so—but now is being persecuted by that world.

Men are out of place. Those who are in high positions do not always qualify for the job, and many times a very intelligent man of wisdom is doing some menial job. Too often, men and women are out of place in their own world.

Then, if you will, Christians are out of place. We have been kicked around. We have to work hard and pray and then fall asleep because we worked all day—and despite our work and our prayers, things do not go right. We are struggling and wandering, and we are just out of place. You belong in the Father's house, but here you are in the devil's house. You are in the world that the devil has temporarily taken over and besmirched. This is our Father's world, but Satan has hijacked it for a period of time.

If we could get Satan where he belongs, sinners where they belong, our Lord where He belongs, Israel where she belongs, the Church where she belongs, men where they belong, and Christians where they belong, we would have that universal harmony after which the whole creation groans. This will happen only in Jesus Christ.

The Living Word's place in this world is to bring purpose to it and bring it together in absolute perfect harmony. The time is coming. The time is at hand. Only in the power of the Holy Spirit can we possibly live up to God's expectation—and it is through the Holy Scriptures that the Holy Spirit empowers us to be all that God desires us to be.

Jesus Christ is calling us to an infinite and eternal triumph of unity and harmony. The final restoration of all God's creation will be in Jesus Christ. We will understand our place in God's universe when we understand the place of Christ—the Living Word—in our world today.

## This Is My Father's World
### Maltbie D. Babcock (1858–1901)

---

This is my Father's world,
And to my listening ears
All nature sings, and round me rings
The music of the spheres.
This is my Father's world;
I rest me in the thought
Of rocks and trees, of skies and seas;
His hand the wonders wrought.

This is my Father's world;
The birds their carols raise.
The morning light, the lily white,
Declare their Maker's praise.
This is my Father's world;
He shines in all that's fair;
In the rustling grass I hear Him pass,
He speaks to me everywhere.

This is my Father's world;
O let me ne'er forget
That though the wrong seems oft so strong,

God is the Ruler yet.
This is my Father's world;
The battle is not done;
Jesus, who died, shall be satisfied,
And earth and heaven be one.

# 4

# THE FIRM FOUNDATION OF THE LIVING WORD

*My heart, O God, beats for Thee and longs for Thy fellowship.*
*By nature, I long for external things far from Thy presence, but the*
*new birth wrought in my heart by the Holy Spirit impels me to*
*seek Thee and call Thee "Abba, Father." My new nature finds*
*harmony and unity in Thy blessed presence. Amen.*

God has established a new covenant, which is not meant to tear down the old covenant—the Old Testament, the old Law—in any way. The old covenant was provisional and laid the foundation for the New Testament. Consider the scaffolding that goes up when erecting a building. You cannot say that the scaffolding is of no benefit. It is of tremendous benefit while the building is being completed. Then, when the building is finished, the scaffolding is torn away. The Old Testament covenant—the Old Testament Law—was scaffolding, provisional for the time until the new building was erected. Then it was old, obsolete and vanished away.

The old covenant was imperfect by the nature of it. It was temporary in its continuance and inadequate in its effect. I will attempt to show here why the Old Testament Law fell short of perfection. By "the Law," I do not mean the Ten Commandments only. God did not give the Ten Commandments by themselves; He gave them as part of a larger law, which included sacrifice, and the priesthood, and the altars and blood, and the lambs and bulls and goats, and the Sabbath. All of these were included when one referred to "the Law."

The Old Testament Law was holy, just and good, but its weakness lay in its location: It was external instead of internal. Always the springs of a man's conduct and character are within him. Jesus said that the outside was not so important; the inside—"That which cometh out of the man" (Mark 7:20)—is what matters. What the Law could never do was change what came out of a man. You can chain a tiger, but it is a tiger still. You can put a mad killer in prison for life, but he is a mad killer until there has been a change on the inside of him. This was the weakness of the Old Testament Law. It could not deal with man's internal motivations. Its directives as to outward behaviors—"Thou shalt not" and "Thou shalt"—could not affect that which was inside of the man.

That which is on the outside is legislation, and you cannot change a man by legislating. The city council could pass a law that requires everybody to love his neighbor, but we cannot fulfill that. We can go grinning down the street and act as though we loved our neighbor in order to stay within the confines of the law and obey the ordinances—and thus stay out of jail. If you smile at your neighbor and look loving, people will probably think you are loving—but that assessment may or may not be accurate. The city council could not pass any such silly law, because you cannot legislate to a man's heart. You can only legislate to a man's conduct. Therefore, the law cannot create any inward moral propensity. This is its weakness.

# Written on Our Hearts

God promised to provide an inward moral bent to holiness. He said that there was to be a new covenant—one that was internal rather than external. The apostle Paul explained it quite clearly: "Forasmuch as ye are manifestly declared to be the epistle of Christ ministered by us, written not with ink, but with the Spirit of the living God; not in tables of stone, but in fleshy tables of the heart" (2 Cor. 3:3).

Now, if you are going to get a new covenant, you make obsolete the old covenant. The old covenant has no moral power over the Christian, because God has made a new covenant with His people, and the Christian is under the new covenant. This new covenant, as we have said, works not from the outside, but from the inside.

In order that we might illustrate this, let us go to nature itself. A young rattlesnake hatches out of its egg, and before it ever sees any other rattlesnake in action, it will coil and strike. When it is just a tiny thing, never having gone to school to learn how to strike, it coils up and strikes. That is a native factor in behavior. It is an action—taken in response to another action—that is not dependent upon individual previous experience.

I have seen chicks hatch out of their shells and lie helpless for maybe five minutes. Then, as a breeze begins to dry them off and a little fluff begins to show, they struggle to their feet—and before they are completely dry, they are out scratching in the dirt. They never saw any chicken scratch. They may as well be the first one ever to do so. They scratch by some native factor that leads them to do acts not dependent upon any previous experience. They do it without having been taught.

This instinctive tendency to action leads to an end. It is that unknown factor that impels each creature—animals, birds, fish, worms, and all the rest—to act like itself. The creature's behavior, of course, can be superficially altered by pressure from the outside.

A chimpanzee can be taught in a circus to put on a bib and eat with a knife and fork, but he is still a chimpanzee. He has not been altered on the inside. His instructors have not in anywise removed that unknown factor that impels every creature to act like itself. He will act like a chimpanzee as soon as he gets by himself or gets with another chimpanzee—because he is a chimpanzee. Forces from the outside have simply pressured and persuaded him to act like something else.

I believe there is such a thing as teaching a sinner to act like a Christian. You baptize him, confirm him, feed him the Lord's Supper regularly, and instruct him in ethics—and after a while, he begins to act like a Christian, just as a chimpanzee acts like a man. However, he is not a Christian, because he has not that inward factor that impels him to righteousness and true holiness. He is only taught from the outside to behave as a Christian.

An overwhelmingly vast number of church members are in this category of having been taught to imitate Christians. They read the Sermon on the Mount and know how a Christian should live. They do not genuinely live like that, but they approximate it. They play it by ear and get close to it—close enough that they are accepted into the church. They attend services and sing and give, and people think they are Christians. Nevertheless, they are living by external pressure and by artificial training and imitation, not by that native factor inside them that teaches them to act in a certain way. They do not have that missing ingredient—that unknown factor that impels them to act like Christians.

Let me take this to extremes in order to clarify. Consider the first archangel in Isaac Watts's (1674-1748) hymn "Eternal

Power, Whose High Abode." While this angel sings, he hides his face beneath his wings:

> There while the first archangel sings,
> He hides his face behind his wings,
> And ranks of shining thrones around
> Fall worshiping, and spread the ground.

Over against him, take that old devil, which is called the "dragon" and "Satan." These two are as far apart morally as I suppose it is possible for creatures to get.

Why does the first archangel act like an archangel? Because of an unknown factor in him compelling him to act like himself. Call it what you will, it is there. When the archangel acts like an archangel, he is not acting the way he has been trained to act; he is acting from the inside out. That thing inside of him makes him do it, and he does not resist it—just as the chick does not resist the urge to scratch. It scratches because something inside of it impels it.

The archangel does not compare himself with somebody else, and say, "Now, I've got to act like an archangel." He acts like an archangel simply because he is an archangel. The Church has long chewed over the question of whether a sinner sins because he is a sinner or is a sinner because he sins. Well, both, of course, are true. He is running in a circle. He sins originally and first because he is a sinner. He is a sinner because he sins. Therefore, he goes around the circle until by the grace of God he breaks out and is a sinner no longer.

Over against the archangel is the devil. He, too, acts like himself, which is the only thing I can say in his favor. Even when he is deceiving, he is acting like himself. Even when he is acting like a devil, he is acting like himself—because he is the devil. Jesus said about certain Jews who were persecuting Him, "Ye are of your father the devil" (John 8:44).

The crowning achievement of the New Testament is to plant in the heart of the believing man an unknown factor that impels him to act righteously. Here lies the difference between denominational churches and true Christianity. It is the difference between training a man to behave like a Christian and having him be born from within a Christian.

The average church is filled with people who have learned the songs of Zion. People who have never been any nearer to God than Adam at his worst will sing some of the most beautiful hymns you ever heard in your life. They got their accent right from Mount Zion. They sing the songs of Israel, but they are not Israelites. They sing the songs of the church, but they are not Christians.

You say, "What right have you got, in this bigoted manner, to rule men out of the church?" I do not have any right to do anything at all; I have the right only to go to hell. But under the grace of God and by the authority granted me by the Lord Jesus Christ, I do have this commission: to draw the line between him who serves God and him who serves Him not, and then to stand and say in His name that unless a man be born again, he cannot enter the kingdom of God.

No amount of training and no religious accent we put on will ever do. The only thing that impels righteous conduct is that something implanted in the human spirit by the Holy Spirit. We call it by various names: the new birth, regeneration or conversion. You are converted in order that you might be regenerated. You are regenerated because you were generated wrong in the first place.

Regeneration—that unknown factor—God calls "My law." He said, "I will put my laws into their mind, and write them in their hearts: and I will be to them a God, and they shall be to me a people" (Heb. 8:10). A Christian, then, is one who has had the laws of God inscribed in his heart, at the motivation center of his life. Nothing else is a Christian.

The New Testament teaches that there will be conflicting factors in even a Christian's life. While the mainstay of his life is that rule of God written not in stone, but in flesh, there are forms of opposition that sometimes overcome him—weakness in the flesh, the world, lust and old habits.

In the seventh chapter of Romans appears a classic wail of a holy man who sometimes felt factors stirring within him, impelling him to be unholy. Paul cried, "O wretched man that I am! who shall deliver me from the body of this death?" (Rom. 7:24). He went on, in the eighth chapter, to show that provision has been made toward deliverance from these wild factors that lie in us, which we call "the flesh" or "carnality" or "the old man"—"for the law of the Spirit of life in Christ Jesus hath made me free from the law of sin and death" (Rom. 8:2).

## Can Religion Be Taught?

In the letter to the Hebrews, we find this statement of the manner in which God's new covenant with His people operates:

> And they shall not teach every man his neighbour, and every man his brother, saying, Know the Lord: for all shall know me, from the least to the greatest. For I will be merciful to their unrighteousness, and their sins and their iniquities will I remember no more (Heb. 8:11-12).

The important consideration is: *Can religion be taught?* A tremendous lot of emphasis is being placed upon what we call

"religious education" in our day. I believe in religious education . . . if we understand what we mean by it. Doctrine and
ethics can be taught. You can get half a dozen little children before you and teach them: "God is love" (1 John 4:8); "God created the heaven and the earth" (Gen. 1:1); "God so loved the
world, that He gave His only begotten Son" (John 3:16); "Believe on the Lord Jesus Christ, and thou shalt be saved" (Acts
16:31). That is doctrine, and you can teach doctrine.

You can also teach ethics—righteous laws. You can get those
little ones before you, and you can teach them: "Obey your parents, lie not, do not steal." We can teach that—and we should.
Doctrine should be taught. Ethics should be taught.

Salvation, however, cannot be taught. Salvation is that which
happens in a man's life because he believes the doctrine he has
heard. Now, a man can hear the doctrine, learn it and pass a
test in it; and recite the catechism from the first to the last, letter perfect; and still not be a Christian, because you cannot by
teaching make a man a Christian—though by teaching, you
can impel him to *want* to be a Christian. You can show him *how*
to be a Christian. Once he has become a Christian, you can
teach him, as Jesus said, "All things . . . whatsoever I have said
unto you" (John 14:26). But you cannot *make* him a Christian
by teaching him.

The curriculum never yet was devised that could cause a
baby to be. Babies are life, born out of life. However, after he is
born and grows up, he can be sent to college and subjected to
curriculum, and he can learn a great deal that he ought to know.

Nevertheless, you have to start with life. You cannot create
life by teaching. I wonder how many so-called Christians are
Christians only by instruction—only by religious education;
only by having somebody manipulate them, put them in water
or sprinkle water on them. It is tragic that we can come into the

Church, take part in it and be known for being Christians, because we are acting like Christians. We do not do this and we do not do the other. We are in church, and we give.

We are somewhat refined. Therefore, we act like Christians, but the terrible thing is that we are Christians by manipulation—by instruction—rather than by regeneration. Salvation, among other things, brings an implantation within the soul of an unknown factor that impels the saved person to act a certain way. The true Christian cries out to the Father by impulse of the Spirit. He does not ask to be taught. Nobody says to the new Christian, "Say, '*Abba* Father.'" He says it because the Spirit of the Son is in his heart, telling him to say it.

The probing question needing an answer is: *Has this happened to me? Have I received Him? Believed on Him? Has He wrought in me this miracle impelling me to want to do right and making me grieve if I don't?* It is imperative that we ask the question and answer it truthfully. It is imperative that we answer it in the affirmative. It would be a heartbreaking—at least a disheartening—thing if we were permitted to stand out in front of the average church and question each one who steps out: "Are you truly a Christian inside? Do you have implanted in you by the miracle of the new birth that unknown factor that God has called His laws—that thing that makes you want to do righteousness and hate sin and love God and hate iniquity? Are you, yourself, blessed with this inward factor that impels to holiness?"

Would you get an honest answer? You would get the brush-off from 99 percent. If you got honest answers, it would be heartbreaking, because there is no question about it. If all the people who go to church had this unknown factor, this thing impelling them to righteousness, this would be a different country from what it is now. "Christian" would be quite some other thing from what it is now.

Let us come before God and say, *Lord, don't let me be one more of these persons who is like the chimpanzee that's been trained to act like a man, but isn't a man, and will die a chimpanzee. Help me, Lord, that I may not be a sinner—a good sinner, a moral sinner, a sinner with high ethical standards, a religious sinner, but a sinner nevertheless.* This would be a terrible tragedy. Only the Holy Spirit through the Word of God can penetrate deep into the soul of man to effect the radical change needed to make a Christian.

## The Church's One Foundation
### Samuel J. Stone (1839–1900)

The Church's one foundation
Is Jesus Christ her Lord;
She is His new creation
By water and the Word.
From heav'n He came and sought her
To be His holy bride;
With His own blood He bought her,
And for her life He died.

Elect from ev'ry nation,
Yet one o'er all the earth,
Her charter of salvation
One Lord, one faith, one birth;
One holy name she blesses,
Partakes one holy food,
And to one hope she presses,
With ev'ry grace endued.

Though with a scornful wonder
Men see her sore oppressed,

By schisms rent asunder,
By heresies distressed:
Yet saints their watch are keeping,
Their cry goes up, "how long?"
And soon the night of weeping
Shall be the morn of song.

'Mid toil and tribulation,
And tumult of her war,
She waits the consummation
Of peace forevermore;
Till with the vision glorious
Her longing eyes are blest,
And the great Church victorious,
Shall be the Church at rest.

Yet she on earth hath union
With God the three in one,
And mystic sweet communion
With those whose rest is won.
O happy ones and holy!
Lord, give us grace that we,
Like them, the meek and lowly,
On high may dwell with Thee.

# 5

# THE AUTHORITY OF GOD RESTS ON THE BIBLE

*Thy Word, O God, has been my meat and drink. I thirst
after Thee and drink deeply of Thy precious Word, as the hart panteth
after the water brooks. I submit myself to Thee and Thine authority
as revealed to me in the Word of God. I have tasted and found
Thee to satiate the inner longing of my heart. May Thy Word be
my strength this day. Amen.*

The subject of the Bible's authority is crucial. As part of my doctrinal creed, I believe in this statement of faith from the Christian and Missionary Alliance:

> The Old and New Testaments, inerrant as originally given, were verbally inspired by God and are a complete revelation of His will for the salvation of men. They constitute the divine and only rule of Christian faith and practice.

Every Protestant throughout the world in every generation believes something similar to this. The Word of God is central to our faith. It is more than just a centerpiece; it is the source of authority, not only in my creedal life but also in my daily life. We are, after all, sons of the Reformation.

The real issue at the beginning of the Reformation was the place of God's Word in the life of the believer. Coming out of the Roman Catholic position were the protesters—or, as they later became known, Protestants. Martin Luther, John Calvin, John Wycliffe, Ulrich Zwingli and John Huss were just a few of the major leaders in the Protestant movement.

Their issue with the Roman Catholic Church had to do with the Bible. Here the battle was fought and won. Unfortunately, we who are the sons of the Reformation have lost sight of the real issue at stake at that time. All other differences were at most secondary—the main focus of the protestors was on the position of the Bible. After all, everything they lived for rested on the authority of the Bible. If this was not God's Word, all else was lost.

The fundamental achievement of the Reformation was not the giving of the Bible to the masses, but rather the establishing of its authority in the Church. This authority was to be above tradition, interpretation, priest or preacher. Nothing was to take precedence over the Word of God. It stands alone and above all other authorities in the world. Everything in the Christian's life and ministry was to flow out of the Word of God under the direction of the Holy Spirit.

Those old men of God would be quite discouraged if they were to come back and see how the authority of God's Word has deteriorated among today's so-called Protestant churches, almost to the point of reversing the tremendous work of the reformers in this area. Certainly, in most of these churches, the Bible has some authority—but not supreme authority.

The authority of God's Word is made subject to interpretation and sometimes even the translation of the Bible, which changes from one generation to another. What one generation agrees to be biblically prohibited, the next generation accepts—

as though truth were flexible and fluid. Keep in mind, whatever is true is not new, and what is new cannot be true.

Even now, the traditions of the church seem to have more authority than the Word of God. But every tradition has a beginning—a time before which it was not done. Then someone did it, and it became a tradition. Today, some are establishing traditions not based upon the clear teaching of the Scriptures—and one generation's tradition becomes the next generation's brazen serpent.

My stand is simply that anything not clearly based on the authority of God's Word does not have God's blessing. This may explain the absence of divine blessing in many evangelical, Protestant churches today. To understand the authority of God's Word from God's perspective, we need to go back to the beginning.

We must start with the authority of the Old Testament.

## God's Perfect Plan

In Judaism God laid a firm foundation for redemption. Nothing was left to chance or caprice; God was very careful to lay down a foundation that would carry on to the cross of Christ and beyond. This foundation was established with an eternal perspective. Everything God does fits into eternity and rings in full harmony with God's will.

God showed Moses His plan for a tabernacle in which He Himself would dwell, and warned him, "Look that thou make them after their pattern, which was shewed thee in the mount" (Exod. 25:40). The plan God laid down did not need any of man's improvements; it was perfect as given by God.

Every generation for some reason feels the need to change or improve upon God's plan. We must purge ourselves of this terrible god-complex in our own generation. We are to accept God's Word as He gave it, regardless of any personal inconvenience. My experience has been that although the Bible is wonderful, it is at the same time, in terms of its demands, the most inconvenient book you can read.

As I have said, God's foundation was not of such a nature as to be improved upon. God made it quite clear to Moses that he was not to expand upon, change or modify any part of the plan. Even those aspects of the plan that did not make sense to man were not to be altered—because it was God's plan, after all, and not offered to man for his critique or approval. It was born in the heart of God, and no man dare infringe upon God's heart.

The message was final; there was to be no amending. When groups get together and have their annual meetings, they like to have amendments. People approve generally of what has been proposed, but they want to add their amendment to it in order to improve or personalize it. God's plan does not need any amendment; it does not require man's approval or any modification to make it easier for any given generation.

Furthermore, there is no room in God's plan for compromising. When He says a thing is or should be a certain way, then that is how it is, regardless of whether it makes sense to us. God has never been in the compromising business, and there is no indication that He intends to begin.

That is how men get along with one another. Each one gives a little here and a little there, and by the time all of that giving has taken place, the lot of them end up with something far removed from what any one of them started with or intended. God is not going to allow man to chip away at His plan—compromising here and compromising there, and ending up with something altogether different from God's original plan.

There is also no room in God's plan for excusing. Some aspects of God's plan seem harsh at first reading. We think of the sacrifices and all of the other difficult things that were in the

Old Testament plan of God. Sometimes we are wont to take what God has done and make excuses. "Oh yes," someone might explain, "God said that, but He really didn't mean it that way." Then comes a long explanation of what that person thinks God really meant. If you have to explain it, you do not believe it. By faith, we can accept from God what we may not understand. That is the dynamic of faith.

God does not need someone to make excuses for His plan as though it had something missing. This plan takes into account every possible consideration and needs no adjustment for the times. Nothing takes God by surprise, and nothing is ever done by God capriciously; He knows the end from the beginning, and all His plans take that into consideration.

The authority of the Old Testament had complete and final jurisdiction over the conscience and the conduct of the people. There was no appeal above it. It determined how men were to act and what would happen to them if their conduct did not align with the Word of God. It was to apply to all without exception. As Paul wrote, "There is no respect of persons with God" (Rom. 2:11).

The message in its finality carried with it the authority of God. Jesus said, "If they hear not Moses and the prophets, neither will they be persuaded, though one rose from the dead" (Luke 16:31). That was an illustration of the authority God gave to the Old Testament. Jesus and the Holy Spirit emphasized that authority in the New Testament. But what good is it to have authority without any personal application?

This brings us to the authority of the New Testament.

## Building on the Foundation

All through the Gospels, we see that Jesus always spoke with authority—not like the scribes and the Pharisees, but with an authority that supersedes human authority: "For he taught them as one having authority, and not as the scribes" (Matt. 7:29). The Old Testament had granted this authority:

> The Lord thy God will raise up unto thee a Prophet from the midst of thee, of thy brethren, like unto me; unto him ye shall hearken; According to all that thou desiredst of the Lord thy God in Horeb in the day of the assembly, saying, Let me not hear again the voice of the Lord my God, neither let me see this great fire any more, that I die not. And the Lord said unto me, They have well spoken that which they have spoken. I will raise them up a Prophet from among their brethren, like unto thee, and will put my words in his mouth; and he shall speak unto them all that I shall command him (Deut. 18:15-18).

The authority under which Jesus operated was established in the Old Testament. What Jesus was doing was a carryover from the Old Testament.

If you read through the book of Acts, you will find it to be a record of Bible preaching in the Early Church. Look at the recorded messages of Peter and Stephen and the apostle Paul, and you will discover how they reasoned, how they taught, and how they appealed to the Old Testament Scripture. There was no New Testament at the time; God's Word to them was the Old Testament.

As they preached the Old Testament, they did so under the authority of Jesus Christ. In Jesus Christ, the Old Testament unfolded all its glory. The Old Testament prepared the way for Christ and transferred to Him all power and all authority. In Christ was the fulfillment of everything that had been established in the Old Testament.

The Church birthed on the day of Pentecost was literally a product of the Word of God. It sprang out of the Scripture and rested upon it for its existence and sustenance. Take the Word of God away from the Church and it ceases to be a movement of God with authority. Sometimes it is easy to forget that spiritual authority does not lie in institutes, colleges or seminaries. Only the Word of God under the direction of the Holy Spirit can empower the Church today.

A review of church history reveals how important the Word of God has been from generation to generation.

For example, the Reformation brought about a renewed commitment to the Word of God, resulting in the conservation of orthodoxy. The main accomplishment of the Reformation was putting the Scriptures, the Word of God, in the center of church life and making it available to all people. The Bible was not just for the elite, but for all who hungered and thirsted after righteousness. Many of the leaders of the Reformation sacrificed their lives making the Word of God available to the people.

After the great Reformation came the revivals. The revivals under the leadership of John and Charles Wesley are most remarkable; these, in effect, took the Bible to the people. Often, because he was not permitted to preach in the churches, John Wesley stood in the open marketplace and proclaimed the Word of the Lord. I am sure he would not have thought of that on his own, but because of the situation it became a necessity. The common people heard him gladly, and out of his ministry flowed a revival that lasted many years and, according to some historians, saved England from collapse.

The problem with the revivals of history is that they have usually been temporary; they are like flashes of lightning—quite dramatic, but illuminating only briefly. I do not mean to take away from their importance; I only wish to point out the fact that the Church of Jesus Christ does not rest upon these dramatic revivals, but rather upon the simple Word of the Lord declared in the power of the Holy Spirit.

Those churches are the truest that stay closest to the Word of God. Even to this day, this is so. Because this fidelity carries a price many are not willing to bear, not all churches remain firmly rooted in the Scriptures.

A similar principle applies to teachers and preachers. Those teachers and preachers most honored are the ones who honored the Word of God the most. I feel it is important that a man in the ministry limit himself to the Scriptures. There are so many other things that may gain a person's attention, so the man of God must constantly focus on the Word of God. When he does so, God invariably gives him authority.

It is by no means easy to maintain this singular focus. The snare of brilliance in the pulpit has been the downfall of many a preacher. Down through the years, mighty orators have risen above the crowd—and unfortunately have also risen "above" the plain teaching of the Scriptures. The pulpit is no place to exhibit a man's brilliance; rather, it is a place simply to declare, "Thus saith the Lord."

The trap many fall into is preaching about the Bible instead of preaching the Bible. This is about the same as a man talking about eating rather than actually eating. No matter how much you talk about eating, it never satisfies the appetite. No matter how much you talk about the Bible, it never ministers to the heart that pants after God. To teach about the Bible instead of teaching the Bible is to substitute a golden calf for the living God. The impostor may look pretty and brilliant and receive many compliments, but it is not the real thing. Happy is the congregation whose pastor knows the difference.

God's judgment upon those who do not preach His Word is that He has left them barren. Here is the danger of taking things for granted—believing that I am preaching the Word when I am only preaching about the Word. It may not seem like much of a difference from a human standpoint, but it means a great deal as far as the Holy Spirit is concerned.

Jesus understood that when He said, "It is the spirit that quickeneth; the flesh profiteth nothing: the words that I speak unto you, they are spirit, and they are life" (John 6:63).

Then we have the awful words of Jesus: "He that rejecteth me, and receiveth not my words, hath one that judgeth him: the word that I have spoken, the same shall judge him in the last day" (John 12:48).

To defy the authority of the Word in our life or ministry is to offend the blessed Holy Spirit, who begins to back off from the person who does so—and from that person's ministry. I, for my part, desire to honor God in my life and ministry by establishing the undisputed authority of God's Word in my life, regardless of the cost or inconvenience.

## A Mighty Fortress Is Our God
### Martin Luther (1483–1546)

A mighty Fortress is our God,
A Bulwark never failing;
Our Helper He, amid the flood
Of mortal ills prevailing.
For still our ancient foe
Doth seek to work us woe;
His craft and power are great,
And armed with cruel hate,
On earth is not his equal.

Did we in our own strength confide,
Our striving would be losing,
Were not the right Man on our side,
The Man of God's own choosing.
Dost ask who that may be?
Christ Jesus, it is He;
Lord Sabaoth, His name,
From age to age the same,
And He must win the battle.

And though this world, with devils filled,
Should threaten to undo us,
We will not fear, for God hath willed
His truth to triumph through us.
The Prince of Darkness grim,
We tremble not for him;
His rage we can endure,
For, lo, his doom is sure;
One little word shall fell him.

That word above all earthly powers,
No thanks to them, abideth;
The Spirit and the gifts are ours,
Through Him who with us sideth.
Let goods and kindred go,
This mortal life also;
The body they may kill;
God's truth abideth still;
His kingdom is forever.

# 6

# Taking the Word
# of God Seriously

*I have heard Thy Word, O Lord, and it has filled my heart
with praise and adoration. Let me never lose sight of the priceless
value of Thy Word in my personal life. Let me never
assume anything, but rather allow the Holy Spirit to confirm in my
life each day Thy blessed will. Amen.*

One great concern I have is that many of today's Christians are
not taking the Word of God seriously. For whatever reason, the
Scriptures do not have authority in the Christian's life in the way
that is necessary for him or her to live a life to the glory of God.
Many have taken to trivializing God's Word; some even treat it as
a sort of game to have some fun. If we are going to be empowered
by the Holy Spirit, we must start by taking the Bible seriously.

Paul explains that "faith cometh by hearing, and hearing by
the word of God" (Rom. 10:17). Apart from the Word of God
and serious attention to it, our faith will flounder in the slough
of despondency.

Perhaps the primary reason for our not taking the Word of
God so seriously is that we have become susceptible to the
many noisy things out in the world that really do not matter.
These things are noisy, I say, yet they do not matter much one
way or another. Even the world talks about them with a sly
wink and does not take them too seriously.

Certainly, there are things in the world that matter, such as hunger, pain, life, death and destiny. These things matter and should be given serious consideration. But apart from these, not much really matters—and it seems that the noisier a thing is, the less it matters. We Christians are like the little baby in a crib; our attention is best held by noisy rattles. In fact, the noisier the rattle, the better we like it.

But let me say again: Just because a thing makes noise does not mean it counts for much.

Politics, regardless of the party, does not really count much. It matters not if you are a Democrat or a Republican. The politics of our country can be changed at the whim of politicians who are only concerned about how they are going to be reelected next time around. Any policy that would hinder their reelection they are adamantly and eloquently against.

Philosophies do not really matter, either. The debate between idealism and realism is really not a matter of life and death. I can have a grand old time discussing the relative merits of various philosophies, and come away exhausted and filled with intellectual pride, but nothing in the world has changed. I can win an argument, but nothing out in the world that really matters is affected by my victory.

Then there is psychology. Neither the old nor the new psychology matters much out in the world. As a young person, I became pretty well schooled in the subject of psychology. I went to lectures, read books, and thought a great deal about the theories of psychology. What I discovered is that after everything has been examined, nothing has really changed. The things that matter out in the world are not affected one sliver by psychology.

Even science, as important as it might be, does not change the things that really matter. We have the Newtons, the Einsteins, and the next brain that will come in order of succession.

After they have said everything they know and lectured learnedly about the newest scientific discovery, nothing that really matters has changed.

Poetry and song are other noisy things that exist in the world but do not bring about change. I love poetry and have read a lot of it in my day. I must confess, much of it is bad poetry, but occasionally I come across a great poet. It is a great day in my life when I discover such a poet. But even after relishing the poetry of this great poet, I find that nothing that really matters has changed.

All of these things pass away and leave us, unchanged, under the pounding blows of life and pain and death.

I will even include preaching in this category. Certainly preaching has its purposes. It is a way to develop social structure, build character, and better a community. It promotes noble manhood and beautiful womanhood, and can even be the influence of lofty thoughts. All of that is good. Many preachers are committed to this kind of preaching, and I acknowledge that there are surface benefits—but after every sermon has been preached, it is only a sound of a far-off voice that tolerates nonsense. None of this is taken seriously, because it is not serious; it does not count in the crisis.

Think about the last sermon that you heard. How important would the lessons of that sermon be if you were in an automobile accident, facing the possibility of death? Some things are matters of life and death; some things do not really matter that much.

## Coming to Terms with the Word of God

This brings me to the one thing that really matters—the one thing we must take seriously. That one thing, of course, is the Bible. I hold in my hand a book, the Bible, and it is above sect, nationality, race, gender, and school of thought. This book I hold in my hand is the one serious book that makes a difference; all others pale in comparison.

I wonder what a person would think who has lived all his life in a cave and finally comes out into the sunlight and sees the sun for the very first time. How would that person describe the sun? What would he really think of the sun? From the day he was born, he has lived without the influence, or so he thinks, of the sun in his life.

What about all those people who have (so they think) lived in a spiritual cave and have never seen the sunlight of God's Word? It is hard to believe that anybody could be in that category. And yet, even in the United States of America, arguably the most Christian nation in the world, there are people who have yet to be exposed personally to the Word of God.

What if such a person were to come to the Word of God for the very first time? He would begin reading and would find that this book makes some rather astounding claims.

First of all, this book we call the Bible stands alone. No other book is comparable, and therefore no other authority casts its shadow on the Bible. My authority as a Christian rests solely upon this book—not upon this book plus some other book.

Additionally, the Bible represents the authoritative Word of God. There can be no straddling the fence or quibbling over shades of meaning. We must accept the Bible on its own terms and not make exceptions for someone who does not quite agree with everything in the Bible. It is either all of the Word of God or none of the Word of God. To slice it up is to compromise its authority.

Now, many delight in taking a slice of Scripture here, a slice there, and a slice over and under; and they develop something that is not really what the Bible teaches. All the cults have done this. Heretics take delight in doing this and trying to convince people that what they are teaching is actually the Bible. But in actuality, it is the Bible manipulated and mangled to fit someone's prejudice or agenda.

If these claims about the Bible are true, then this book deserves our earnest attention—for it affects us in life, pain, death and destiny.

Yet, some still refuse to take it seriously.

I can see only two possibilities of why people do not take the Bible seriously.

## Is the Bible False?

The first possibility is that you have discovered the Bible to be false. After reading the Scriptures, studying the Scriptures, examining the Scriptures, and comparing Scripture with Scripture, you have ascertained that the Bible simply is not true. This presupposes that you have examined, weighed, searched and labored over the problem until you have exhausted every resource and have come to the inarguable conclusion that the Bible is false.

I am amazed that the biggest critics of the Bible are those who have never really studied the Bible. This approach would not be tolerated in the worlds of medicine or science, or in the legal profession, to give just a few examples. Imagine if somebody who had never read any kind of medical theory criticized the latest developments in medicine. That person would be disclaiming something as being false, and yet he would not be able to explain why it is false. Such a person would never be taken seriously in the medical community.

So these critics of the Bible rant and rave about the authenticity and authority of the Bible and yet have no logical arguments to back up their ranting. They question the authorship of the Bible but offer no reasonable explanation for their position.

Let us for a moment assume that it is possible to come to the point of being certain—after, as I said, doing much research and study of the Scriptures—that the Bible is false. What effect does that have?

To start with, it disillusions all who have been transformed through the power and authority of the Word of God, all those people who were struggling in life—maybe even finding themselves on skid row somewhere—and then were dramatically transformed by reading the Bible. Perhaps someone read the Scriptures to them and prayed with them, and as a consequence of their believing the Word of God, their lives were completely changed. What they once were they no longer are. One could fill a book (or a series of books) with the testimonies of the multiplied thousands that have been so transformed by the Word of God.

Now someone comes along and tells these individuals that the Bible is false. How does that affect them? Do they say something like, "This man says that the Bible is false. Therefore, my conversion and transformation are false. Nothing really happened to me. I'm the same person I used to be." What a ridiculous thing to think, when the transformation is evident to all.

Men who claim that the Bible is false are insinuating that all those people whose lives have been changed by it are living in delusion. Oh, may more people be so delusional! I have known such men and women, and I know exactly what they would say. They would repeat the words of the blind man, who said to the Pharisees who questioned the reality of who Jesus was, "Whether he be a sinner or no, I know not: one thing I know, that, whereas I was blind, now I see" (John 9:25). It was hard to question the authority of Jesus Christ when before the Pharisees stood this man who once was blind but now could see.

Then there is the area of works of mercy. The unbeliever's claim that the Word of God is not the Word of God not only disillusions those who have been transformed, but also unravels the works of mercy done in the name of Jesus.

Usually a great work of mercy begins with someone who has been radically transformed by the Word of God—a person who has genuinely been converted to Jesus Christ. Such a person then reaches out to those who are unfortunate—to those who are in situations such as he was before he encountered the Christ of the Bible—and shows them mercy and kindness through his actions in their behalf.

If these who do not believe in the authority of the Bible are right, then we need to close all of the asylums and leper colonies, the missionary works in some of the most primitive areas of the world, and the hospitals that have been used so greatly to ease the suffering of humanity. Are these who disbelieve the Word of God prepared to tell us that unbelief created all of these works of mercy?

If the Bible is false, who gets credit for the compassionate actions of those who are living out its precepts?

Then, what about all the believers who have dramatically influenced society down through the years? If the Bible is false, as some declare it to be, then we need to give booby prizes and dunce caps to these believers who built their lives on the Word of God—even if, out of their efforts, there came a powerful influence for godliness.

I'm talking about people like Francis Bacon, William Gladstone, Michelangelo, Pascal, Spinoza, Milton—and the list goes on and on. If the Bible is false, then these men were fools. Their biographies record that they gave credit to almighty God for His work in their lives and accepted the authority of the Holy Scriptures. Certainly, they did not all believe alike in everything, but the focus of their lives was on the authority of God's Word. They were very serious in their approach to the Scriptures.

In my mind, one of the great books of all time is *Foxe's Book of Martyrs*, by John Foxe. But what fools these men and women were, if the Bible is not the inspired, authoritative Word of God! Why would anybody be so foolish as to give up his life, the most precious thing he has, for something that is false?

If the Bible could be proved false, that would be a terrible thing with far-reaching consequences—but no serious-minded, scholarly person who has given time and thought to the study of the Bible would ever come to the conclusion that it is false. To do so presumes that you know more than God—or, worse yet, that God is deliberately holding something good back.

## Trifling with the Word of God

If a person has not determined the Bible is false—if he in fact knows it to be true—and yet does not take it seriously, he is guilty of trifling with the Word of God. If we believe that the Bible is God's Word to us, then it needs to have top priority in all our activities. Everything we do must be evaluated according to "thus saith the Lord." The serious-minded Christian should discard completely anything that does not measure up to this standard.

To trifle with something as important as the Bible is the epitome of foolishness. Let me say right here that I do not believe the Bible to be a religious book. There have been many religious books down through the years, and I have read most of them. Every religion—every cult—has their religious book. The religious book is a list of do's and don'ts that must be followed if you are part of that religion.

Some people look at the Bible as a list of do's and don'ts. To do so is to stop short of the integrity of the Bible. There is an old hymn that we sang in church, titled, "Break Thou the Bread of Life." I love that hymn, particularly a phrase in the first verse: "Beyond the sacred page, I seek Thee, Lord." To look at the Bible as anything other than a "sacred page" through which God exercises His authority is to trivialize it to our own spiritual detriment.

I solemnly vow before God Almighty that every day of my life, I will take the Bible as the most serious thing and adjust my life to its teachings.

## Break Thou the Bread of Life
### Mary A. Lathbury (1841–1913)

Break Thou the bread of life,
Dear Lord, to me,
As Thou didst break the loaves
Beside the sea;
Beyond the sacred page
I seek Thee, Lord;
My spirit pants for Thee,
O Living Word.

Bless Thou the truth, dear Lord,
To me, to me,
As Thou didst bless the bread
By Galilee;
Then shall all bondage cease,
All fetters fall;
And I shall find my peace,
My All in all.

Thou art the Bread of Life,
O Lord, to me,
Thy holy Word the truth
That saveth me;
Give me to eat and live
With Thee above;
Teach me to love Thy truth,
For Thou art love.

O send Thy Spirit, Lord,
Now unto me,
That He may touch my eyes
And make me see;
Show me the truth concealed
Within Thy Word,
And in Thy book revealed
I see the Lord.

# PART II

. . . . . . . . . . . . . . .

# OBSTRUCTIONS TO GOD'S POWER

*This is my comfort in my affliction:*
*for thy word hath quickened me.*

PSALM 119:50

# 7

# DEALING WITH THE GREAT SPIRITUAL DECEPTION

*There is a blindness, O Father, which permeates deep into the soul of a man, obscuring Thy face. The world is against me. My flesh is in conspiracy against my soul. And the enemy of my soul strives to keep me from the blessed light of the gospel. May my heart be overwhelmed by the brightness of Thy smile. May Thy light chase away forever the spiritual darkness that encumbers my relationship with Thee. In Jesus' name. Amen.*

One thing that should encourage the heart of every Christian is that God has not left this world of ours without light. The whole tenor of scriptural teaching points to Jesus as the light "which lighteth every man that cometh into the world" (John 1:9). God, in His infinite wisdom, has established Jesus as the light of the world.

Apart from Jesus, men stumble in the shadow of their own rebellion. Under the influence of the Prince of Darkness, they continue to walk in darkness as deep, dangerous and hopeless as if the light had never come. Look at some people: There is a sense of hopelessness about them—and yet before them is the hope of the world, even the Lord Jesus Christ. What causes a person to deliberately turn away from the light and walk in the shadow of his own darkness? Why are his eyes so blind to the brilliance of Jesus Christ, who indeed is the light of the world?

From a natural point of view, a blind man carries his darkness in his eyes. For the blind man, there may be day all around him, but there is only deep midnight in his eyes. The light, to a blind man, is of no value; he may even deny that it exists. As far as he is concerned, the light does not exist. No matter how much you try to convince him, he does not possess the ability to see the light. He wallows in his own blindness, helplessly.

I believe that the same is true spiritually. Even though the light of the gospel shines all around them, men and women still choose to walk in the blindness of their own hearts. They emphatically deny that there is such a thing as light. Or, choosing to walk in spiritual darkness, they despise the light. No matter how beneficial the light may be, people still choose the darkness. "And this is the condemnation, that light is come into the world, and men loved darkness rather than light, because their deeds were evil" (John 3:19).

I want to point out that this spiritual blindness, unlike natural blindness, is self-induced. Today there is really no excuse for spiritual blindness. With all the advances in technology, very few people are actually far from the light of the gospel. With radio, television and other forms of media, there is not a single minute of the day when the gospel is not being presented. No other generation has enjoyed such light as the present one—and by the same token, no other generation has despised such light.

We have the advancement of all kinds of light these days. Social light, political light, scientific light, and on I could go. The only light that is being neglected is the spiritual light.

Spiritual blindness may take many forms. For instance, there are some who pervert the gospel light, twisting the truth for their own gain. Too many are eager to take advantage of people by means of religion, and too many people are prone to be vulnerable in this area.

In spite of all this, there still are many avenues in our society today through which the gospel of Jesus Christ is proclaimed. The world is our mission field, and modern technology is an excellent means to penetrate this mission field with the blessed light of the gospel of Jesus Christ.

One must be careful with technology and media, however. Despite the urgency of the hour to shed abroad the light of the gospel, many are caught up in entertainment, bright lights and tinkling bells. This superficiality is among us to stay. I might as well admit it, even though I do not like it. All of these things are easy and require only human effort. The light that the world needs to know—the light of the gospel—can only be communicated and demonstrated through the power of the Holy Spirit.

## Consequences of Spiritual Blindness

Jesus said, "I am come a light into the world, that whosoever believeth on me should not abide in darkness" (John 12:46). Let me repeat that spiritual blindness is self-induced. Each of us has been given the opportunity to escape the darkness by way of faith in Jesus Christ. Should we opt to remain in the darkness rather than walk in the light, we bring on ourselves the consequences of this choice—the most grievous of which manifest as the presence of certain evil tendencies among humanity.

One consequence of spiritual blindness is hatefulness. Some people are so full of hate, anger and bitterness you can see it in their eyes. Many unresolved issues in life lead to this kind of hatred and bitterness. The blindness of their hearts has allowed the hatred to emanate from their eyes. This is not a psychological problem to be fixed with therapy, but a spiritual problem that needs the blessed light of the gospel to bring transformation.

Another consequence of spiritual blindness is greed. You can look at some people and see greed shining out all over the place. All they think about is what they can get, and how they can take advantage of a situation or person, and how they can get ahead. The spiritual darkness has so shrouded their hearts that all they can think of is taking advantage of the situation at hand. Blindness is horrific when it prevents you from seeing beyond yourself and your self-interest.

Pride in the eyes is another aspect of this spiritual darkness. The Scriptures call it the "pride of life," and such it is. I am amazed by the things people take pride in these days. Most of the time, these things are superficial, transitory accomplishments or honors that really do not matter. People will take pride in winning some basketball game, or in various other achievements that do not change or improve anyone's life in any way. People today take pride in things that would have shamed a former generation. The spiritual darkness keeps us from recognizing what is important and what is not. We have on this generation the curse of the superficial.

Lust in the eyes is another great calamity of the destruction of the spiritual optic nerves. Jesus warned, "But I say unto you, That whosoever looketh on a woman to lust after her hath committed adultery with her already in his heart" (Matt. 5:28).

Lust is the ultimate focus on carnal appetite and appeasement, and it is the foundation of many sins. It is not so much the deed as it is the intention of the heart. An eye full of lust is the great characteristic of this generation, which is most evident as you walk down the streets of any city. Lustful looking. Lustful gazing. Every sin begins with the seed of lust and then flourishes into actions of iniquity. "For all that is in the world," the beloved apostle John said, "the lust of the flesh, and the lust of the eyes, and the pride of life, is not of the Father, but is of the world" (1 John 2:16).

John exhorts us to seek the Father, and to shun the world and all its accoutrements. It is the light of the gospel that guides us toward the Father's heart and away from the world.

Then we have unbelief in the eye. Spiritual darkness results in the curse of unbelief. Unbelief prevents us from coming to the Father through the Son and pushes us away from the kingdom of God, thrusting us out into the kingdom of this world. Nothing is worse than unbelief, because it keeps us from what God has in mind for us.

Revenge is also seen in the eyes of some spiritually blind people. Somebody did something to them, or said something to them, and revenge filled their eyes. They now look for ways to get even with whoever hurt them. Revenge leads to dismay and disheartened feelings, and it is not the way of the genuinely converted. "Dearly beloved," Paul pleads, "avenge not yourselves, but rather give place unto wrath: for it is written, Vengeance is mine; I will repay, saith the Lord" (Rom. 12:19).

The Pharisees exemplified another consequence of spiritual blindness: self-righteousness. They looked down on everyone as being inferior to them. They were the self-imposed standard of what was right and good, holding themselves up as the epitome of righteousness. Everybody else was wrong and needed to measure themselves against the Pharisees. Self-righteousness has probably done more harm to the kingdom of God than anything else. It attempts to replace the righteousness of God with the righteousness of man, which is not righteous at all. There was only one righteous, and that was the Lord Jesus Christ. Eyes of self-righteousness blaspheme the righteousness of Christ.

Yet another consequence of spiritual blindness is rebellion. The focus of this rebellion is God. The great calamity of a spiritually dark optic nerve is that it rebels against God and His authority. Logically, rebellion does not make sense. Nothing good comes from rebellion, especially in the spiritual realm. Rebellion leads us away from God and drives us into the arms of the enemy of man's soul. This rebellion started when Lucifer said, "I will be like the Most High." He injected this poisonous spirit of rebellion into humanity through Eve in the garden. All of humanity has been in rebellion against God since.

Sadly, many have become acclimated to the spiritual darkness within. But this internal blindness carries with it dire consequences. It is responsible for all the pain and misery in our world today. Many blame God for pain, but in reality, our rebellion against God has created all the pain.

This confusion about who is responsible for our pain stems from the fact that the spiritually blind person, afflicted with a perverted conscience, cannot see moral values. Again, there is no logic to this sort of thing. This inner blindness has no way of appreciating a pure conscience and good moral values. What the spiritually darkened call good is contrary to what God calls good. They call good "bad" and bad "good" because of their inward blindness.

## Separated from God and His Kingdom

In my mind, the greatest consequence of people's inward blindness is the fact that they cannot know God and Christ in any intimate sense. Do we need to go further? Unless I can know God and His Son, the Lord Jesus Christ, nothing else really matters. Spiritual blindness prohibits me from piercing the spiritual darkness and coming into the light—the blessed light of knowing God and Jesus Christ.

The kingdom of God is all around us, but those who have internal blindness are unable to see this kingdom and its values. Because the values of God's kingdom are far removed from their perception, they make up their own values based upon their own understanding. They assume that what they believe to be right and wrong is in concert with God's values. After all, they aspire to be like the Most High.

This inner blindness has another consequence that is most disturbing: People so afflicted cannot be sure that they see the Bible aright. Is the Bible really God's Word? What about some of the errors in the Bible? What about all the different translations? Surely, the Bible is not a book that can be trusted. The person who is spiritually blind is not able to be sure about the Word of God and therefore becomes victimized by the purveyors of false doctrine.

When a person can see the Word of God clearly, recognize its authority, and understand God's kingdom, that person can never be led into false doctrine. It is the light of the glorious gospel shed upon our hearts that enables us to see the truth and walk in that truth. All of the heretics or false teachers have congregations whose members are inwardly blinded to the point where they cannot see and understand the Word of God. Easily are such people duped into believing false doctrine.

All this internal blindness exposes a person to fatal self-deception. The worst kind of deception is self-deception. It leads to hell a man who believes himself to be on his way to heaven. "Oh," says the self-deceived, "there are many roads that lead to heaven." Then that deceived person believes he is in fact on the road to heaven. How the devil must delight in this deception, if the devil experiences any delight.

Not just wicked men, but good ones as well, can be inwardly blinded to the point of self-deception. Yes, even good men and women can be so deceived as to miss heaven in the final analysis. How tragic to live your whole life believing you are on the road to heaven, and then to find out, when you cannot change, that you were deceived!

Remember these words spoken by Jesus: "Not every one that saith unto me, Lord, Lord, shall enter into the kingdom of heaven; but he that doeth the will of my Father which is in heaven. Many will say to me in that day, Lord, Lord, have we not prophesied in thy name? and in thy name have cast out devils? and in thy name done many wonderful works? And then will I profess unto them, I never knew you: depart from me, ye that work iniquity" (Matt. 7:21-23).

## The Cure for Spiritual Blindness

How are we to avoid hearing these dreadful words? Surely, there is something we can do to prevent ourselves from being deceived. What is the cure? How am I to deal with any kind of spiritual blindness I might encounter?

Take heart—there is a cure. "For ye were sometimes darkness," Paul wrote to the Ephesian Christians, "but now are ye light in the Lord: walk as children of light" (Eph. 5:8). These men and women once walked in darkness, but they came to walk as children of light. At the root of this transformation was a personal encounter with the Holy Spirit through the Word of God.

Jesus is the cure, and only the Holy Spirit can apply this remedy to restore a person's life and chase away the darkness of the soul forever.

"The Spirit of the Lord is upon me," Jesus proclaimed, "because he hath anointed me to preach the gospel to the poor; he hath sent me to heal the brokenhearted, to preach deliverance to the captives, and recovering of sight to the blind, to set at liberty them that are bruised" (Luke 4:18). Light is available to all who seek. That is the secret. Those who seek God earnestly and desperately shall surely come into the glorious light of His presence.

## The Light of the World Is Jesus
### Philip P. Bliss (1838–1876)

---

The whole world was lost
In the darkness of sin;
The Light of the world is Jesus!
Like sunshine at noon-day
His glory shone in;
The Light of the world is Jesus!

No darkness have we
Who in Jesus abide;
The Light of the world is Jesus!
We walk in the light
When we follow our Guide;
The Light of the world is Jesus!

Ye dwellers in darkness
With sin-blinded eyes,
The Light of the world is Jesus!
Go, wash at His bidding,
And light will arise;
The Light of the world is Jesus!

No need of the sunlight
In Heaven we're told;

The Light of the world is Jesus!
The Lamb is the Light
In the city of gold;
The Light of the world is Jesus!

Come to the light,
'Tis shining for thee;
Sweetly the light
Has dawned upon me.
Once I was blind,
But now I can see:
The Light of the world
Is Jesus!

# 8

# THE NEVER-ENDING BATTLE FOR THE MIND

*Heavenly Father, I am weary of the insidious attacks of
the enemy trying to drive a wedge between Thee and me.
My only solace from this spiritual warfare is Thy counsel given
me in the Holy Scriptures. As I bathe my mind in Thy promises,
I discover a freedom from the tyranny of the enemy of my soul.
I thank Thee for Thy counsel leading me away from the
world and deep into the heart of God. Amen.*

Throughout the Scriptures—both the Old and the New Testaments—two counsels operate in opposition to each other. They are at war with each other for the human mind, each fighting for control of this most godlike treasure. In our world of strife, this is the greatest battle.

Somebody is controlling your mind. The question is: *Who?*

Before we can address this question, I need to explain what I mean by the human mind. The mind is the whole intelligent and moral personality of a person. This includes reason, moral perception, thought, imagination, and the mental and moral responses to events around us. The human mind is an instrument of fearful power and awesome potential, because it determines the conduct, character and final destiny of an individual, nations and the race of mankind. Nothing in God's entire created world can compare to the human mind.

Yet, for all its power, the human mind is helpless by itself; it is controlled by counsel. It may be diluted, blinded, victimized and led astray by bad counsel—we see examples of this every day. I believe each person has the same potential, but not every person realizes the full potential of his mind. A person may be led astray from realizing his potential by dabbling in nonessentials, many of which we have already discussed.

On the other end of the spectrum, the human mind can be raised to heights of purest immortality. Read history and biography, and you will find men and women who rose up, challenged and changed their generations—people who are remembered for all of history.

The fate of the human mind depends upon what kind of counsel it receives. Depending on that counsel, it can be led to depraved depths or immortal heights.

Now, let me explain what I mean by counsel. I mean that moral and intellectual pressure that contributes to the determination of which direction a life shall take. Many pressures are vying to fill that role.

Somebody will protest and say, "I believe in a free mind." The only reason you believe in a free mind is that you have been subjected to some power that has pressured you in that direction. You really did not come up with that on your own.

The human mind, I say, is substantially dependent upon counsel. It is like a musical instrument. The piano, for instance, can play the demoralizing macabre music of death or a triumphant doxology of immortal life. The piano has 52 white keys and 36 black keys, for a total of 88 keys. No matter what song or style of music you want to play, you have at your fingertips the same number of keys. The style of the music will be dependent upon the one who pushes those keys—who puts pressure on a certain sequence of keys.

The musician at the piano determines the kind of music that will come from the instrument. The same is true of our mind. Whoever is putting the pressure on our mind at any particular time is establishing our thinking and influencing the direction in which we will next go.

The mind is like a field of rich, fertile soil. This field can produce briars, thorns and other such useless weeds that really do not profit. Or, it can produce sweet fruit and grain blessed by the rising sun. It is the same soil, under the same sun, but it produces different things. The difference lies in the seed that is planted in that field.

## Slavery of the Mind

There is a war going on to enslave the human mind. The enemy of man's soul will stop at nothing to capture and control the thinking of men and women in our generation. If he can control their thinking, he can control their destiny, which is his objective. In his efforts to determine the fate of mankind, the enemy—Satan himself—employs two kinds of slavery.

There is first the slavery of the body, whereby somebody controls a person's conduct by physical force. This is, perhaps, the easiest slavery Satan has over men. The addictions of our generation and culture have brought millions of people into bondage. Just when one addiction seems to be under control, three others jump up to ravage a generation. The victim knows his condition and longs for personal freedom, but he is so ensnared in his addiction that deliverance seems impossible.

Then there is the slavery of the mind, which is the controlling of a person's mind by means of ideas supplied to it. This is a more subtle form of bondage and is therefore much more dangerous than the slavery of the body. When somebody is addicted to some substance, it is evident to everybody around him or her. However, when the mind is being controlled by ideas from the outside, it can be very difficult to detect. This is the covert strategy of the enemy to dominate a person or persons. Whole cultures are being dominated by false ideas that are accepted without tangible proof. People who are under bondage themselves propagate these ideas without ever understanding their role in the deception.

The dynamic here is that obedience is rendered willingly. People are not coerced into obeying a certain line of thought. In fact, some believe they came up with the ideas themselves. So subtle is the enemy of man's soul. The tragedy is that the victim is unaware of being controlled; he willingly allows something exterior to mold and direct his mind.

The enemy propagates his counsel through every technique and method imaginable: the media, education, modern psychology, radio, television, music, advertising, and many more. His objective is to regiment every living soul to think the thoughts of the ungodly in life, morals, love, God, religion, wealth, work, marriage, the future, death and eternity. All just one happy family, everyone thinking the same thoughts. How convenient for the enemy, and how terrible for that culture.

## The Two Counsels

The only difference in human minds is the effective pressure being exerted on them at the time. Whoever brings pressure to bear upon your mind will determine your values and the direction you are going.

Two counsels—the counsel of the ungodly and the counsel of the Lord—vie for control of the human mind. These two counsels are diametrically opposed to each other. You cannot have a little bit of one and a little bit of the other. It is an either/or situation. Either you are following the counsel of the world or you are following the counsel of the Lord. These counsels lead in opposite directions. You cannot go east at the same time you are going west. You must go in one direction or another, and the counsel you follow will determine that direction. So which counsel are you listening to?

## The Counsel of the Ungodly

First, let us consider the counsel of the ungodly, which leads to a life of wickedness and debauchery when it is followed. I would like to define the counsel of the ungodly generally as the mindset of those who do not give God His proper place in their life. I believe this is where it begins. It then can go to the depths of wickedness and depravity, such as we are seeing in our generation. In my opinion, each generation discovers a new low in this area of depravity in a downward spiral.

What exactly is this ungodly counsel? How should we describe it?

Simply put, it is the counsel of the natural—or un-renewed—man. This man has not been regenerated and is still walking in the shadowy swamps of depravity. I will give you that the unregenerate man can soar very high on intellectualism, philosophy, poetry, and even religion. Ungodly counsel simply means a way of thinking that does not include God on His terms. This is an important point. The unregenerate man will gladly take bits and pieces of God that are amenable to him, but he will not take God on His terms.

I must say right here that God never negotiates with men. Jesus Christ's death on the cross put an end to any kind of negotiations. It is now Christ or nothing. It is now God's Word in its entirety or nothing. The unregenerate man loves to take the Word of God and cherry pick pieces that he does not see as harmful—pieces like, "love your neighbor" or "respect people, especially your parents." There is nothing wrong with these things, but they are only slivers of God's truth.

The unregenerate man employing ungodly counsel will pick and choose which parts of God's Word he will accept, but ungodly counsel will never listen to "thus saith the Lord." The unregenerate man refuses to bow to the authority of God's Word.

This counsel of the ungodly becomes the propaganda in our culture. It sets up a pressure, which directs the lives of men. It seems harmless and on the surface even looks good. But it does not go far enough, and as a result, what it actually does is direct people away from God. We live in a day and age of propaganda. Everything is affected by this propaganda mindset.

Propaganda tells you what toothpaste to buy. Now, in my humble opinion, toothpaste is toothpaste, but if you listen to the propaganda, you will be told that this one particular toothpaste is superior to everything else. The public comes to believe that, and people go out and buy that particular toothpaste. The pressure exerted by propaganda seeks to control everything in our life—from what we do and where we go to what we purchase and how we feel about social issues.

The propaganda machine puts men and women in public office. As we should have learned from Adolf Hitler, propaganda does not necessarily adhere to the truth. Hitler's propaganda philosophy was that if you said something long enough and loud enough, people would begin to believe that it was true. That is the core of propaganda. If you say a thing loud enough and long enough and in the right context, people will believe it to be true, and it will get into our books and our educational system.

Unfortunately, this idea has come hopping and skipping into the Church of Jesus Christ. No other generation has been as committed to propaganda as this generation. Personally, I do not believe that the gospel of Jesus Christ is conducive to propaganda methods. The gospel is not true because we say convincingly that it is; it is true because "thus saith the Lord."

In the hands of ungodly counselors, propaganda becomes a creed, an ideal and the right thing to do. Nobody is more religious than a propagandist. The secret of propaganda is preaching something long enough that people begin to believe that it is true and adjust their life to it.

Ungodly counsel is ubiquitous, contagious and all but irresistible. By that I mean simply that it works. It sells merchandise. It elects politicians. It even fills churches. If you have the right propaganda, you can do anything you want to do. You have the power to control the way that men and women think about something or anything. This power is exercised through conversation, literature, the theater and movies, the press and, of course, through radio and television. Much of our industry in America would collapse if it were not for the terrible power of propaganda. Ungodly counsel depends upon this power of propaganda to survive.

Propaganda controls the minds of every man, regardless of how he may boast of his freedom. Some claim that they are free thinkers, but they came to that conclusion because of certain propaganda. There is only one exception to this; I am speaking of those who rebel against the ungodly counsel and take the counsel of the Lord.

## Untruths Perpetuated by Ungodly Counsel

The counsel of the ungodly—the counsel of unbelief rooted in the heart of every unregenerate man and woman—has a fatal miscalculation. It assumes the permanent value of visible things. There is no consideration given to anything invisible, but everything visible and tangible has, according to their calculations, lasting value. Where this notion comes from is hard to understand. If you have been around for some time, you realize that few things are permanent. There is a constant deterioration of everything visible around us. Around the house, for instance, there are always things that need to be repaired or replaced, because nothing is permanent.

Those who follow the counsel of the ungodly live as if this were the only world.

The propaganda of ungodly counsel sets up a moral pressure away from God. It becomes a custom and a way of life. The natural man is unable to resist this propaganda, which gets its terrible power by brainwashing.

Ungodly counsel assumes the permanence of earthly things and the soundness of un-renewed human nature.

It is the counsel of tolerance, teaching the brotherhood of all men and forgetting the intolerance of the Bible and Christ. Nobody was more intolerant than Jesus Christ was. Just read His teachings (see Matt. 6:24; Luke 14:27). Jesus exhibited an intolerant attitude toward the religious leaders of his day. He said in John 8:44:

> Ye are of your father the devil, and the lusts of your father ye will do. He was a murderer from the beginning and abode not in the truth, because there is no truth in him. When he speaketh a lie, he speaketh of his own: for he is a liar, and the father of it.

That doesn't sound to me like some soft "let's just get along" tolerance for everybody.

Ungodly counsel is also the counsel of the un-crucified flesh. It coddles self and avoids the self-sacrifice of the cross at all cost.

It is the counsel of wickedness that tolerates excuses, overlooks sin, and ignores moral accountability. No matter how wicked a person might be, he always has a reason for doing what he did. In his own mind, those reasons, whatever they might be, excuse him from any personal accountability.

It is the counsel of the flesh, favoring the carnal appetites of man and making no provision for the Spirit of God. Every decision is based upon some fleshly appetite, moving the person ever further in the direction of his carnal desires.

This counsel of the ungodly betrays the welfare of the individual, keeping him from the wise counsel of God.

## The Counsel of the Lord

Then we come to the counsel of the Lord:

O earth, earth, earth, hear the word of the LORD (Jer. 22:29).

Thy word is a lamp unto my feet, and a light unto my path (Ps. 119:105).

Wherewithal shall a young man cleanse his way? by taking heed thereto according to thy word (Ps. 119:9).

Read Proverbs 2:1-9; 4:1-13. The counsel of the Lord is the counsel of wisdom. It will answer the four age-old questions: *What am I? Whence came I? Why am I? Whither go I?* These questions demand specific answers that only come from the counsel of the Lord.

The counsel of wisdom also answers the question, *What shall I do that I may have eternal life?*

The counsel of the Lord is the counsel of eternity; it shall stand forever. The counsel of the Lord shall stand when your life, the human race and even time shall be no more:

> And sware by him that liveth for ever and ever, who created heaven, and the things that therein are, and the earth, and the things that therein are, and the sea, and the things which are therein, that there should be time no longer (Rev. 10:6).

It is the counsel of purity, making no terms with pollution of any kind—which is all but impossible in modern society. The ungodly counsel we find all around us contradicts this counsel of purity. We live in a society of impurity, which is one of the signs of ungodliness. The counsel of purity emphasizes separation from the world and a radical attachment to Jesus Christ.

The counsel of purity will solve the urgent problems of social corruption, crime, delinquency, divorce and personal purity. Deal with these factors and human society blossoms as a rose in a well-tended garden. The counsel of purity will extract from this world the infectious poison of sin.

The counsel of purity comes along and makes men and women clean: "Now ye are clean," Jesus said, "through the word which I have spoken unto you" (John 15:3). There is no other cleansing available but that which comes "through the Word." This indeed is the counsel of the Lord to bring into the lives of redeemed men and women the essence of purity—not purity approved of by the world but rather a purity that is the standard of God.

The counsel of the Lord is the counsel of peace. We live in a world full of distressed hearts, troubled consciences, pills, psychiatrists, and books about positive thinking. None of our endeavors seems to be producing the peace that the human heart insatiably craves.

The counsel of the Lord deals with the conflict in human nature—the conflict between eternity in our hearts and mortality in our hands. The counsel of the Lord shall stand forever.

The counsel of the Lord effectively transforms our thinking, leading us away from the world and into the bosom of Him who loved us and gave Himself for us. Every person's life is a reflection of the counsel he has submitted to and allowed to shape his priorities and interests. Blessed is the man who has submitted, unreservedly, to the counsel of the Lord.

## Abiding and Confiding
### Albert B. Simpson (1843–1919)

I have learned the wondrous secret
Of abiding in the Lord;
I have found the strength and sweetness
Of confiding in His word;
I have tasted life's pure fountain,
I am drinking of His blood,
I have lost myself in Jesus,
I am sinking into God.

I am crucified with Jesus,
And He lives and dwells in me,
I have ceased from all my struggling,
'Tis no longer I but He;
All my will is yielded to Him,
And His Spirit reigns within,

And His precious blood each moment
Keeps me cleansed and free from sin.

All my cares I cast upon Him,
And He bears them all away;
All my fears and griefs I tell Him,
All my needs from day to day.
All my strength I draw from Jesus,
By His breath I live and move;
E'en His very mind He gives me
And His faith and life and love.

For my words I take His wisdom,
For my works His Spirit's pow'r,
For my ways His gracious presence
Guards and guides me every hour;
Of my heart He is the Portion,
Of my joy the ceaseless Spring,
Savior, Sanctifier, Keeper,
Glorious Lord and loving King.

I'm abiding in the Lord,
And confiding in His word,
And I'm hiding, safely hiding,
In the bosom of His love.

# 9

# WHEN FACING
# THE LETHAL LIE

*O Jesus, Thou living Truth from which all truth flows, I honor
Thee in my life this day. May I not become diverted from Thy truth
by the ingenious lies the enemy has put forth. By Thy blessed Holy
Spirit may I delve into Thy Word—Thy living Word—by which my
heart and mind and life are fixed on the Lord Jesus Christ, and I am
transformed into His image day by day. Amen.*

The human mind is of such a nature that deception is easily
practiced upon it. Even being in possession of a great store of
knowledge is no assurance that you will not be deceived. The
most dangerous attitude anybody can have is that which says: *I
know so much that I cannot be deceived.* This attitude has led many
people down the path to deception.

When a person is deceived, he is likely to make errors. An
engineer, for example, can be deceived by having wrong information, which will cause errors in his design. Those errors can
cause that new building or bridge to be unsound and prone to
collapse. A doctor can be deceived as to the meaning of medical
test results—and then make an error in his diagnosis. The consequences of that can be quite devastating.

As potentially dangerous as these things are, the consequences of errors caused by deception are more terrible when it
comes to religion. For these errors affect not only this life but

also the life to come. Anything touching eternity has to be handled very carefully. When dealing with eternity, we need to make sure we have truth that has filtered out any and all errors. The human heart has a deep aversion to naked Bible truth. In order for the human heart to be attracted to biblical truth, it must be "jazzed up" a little bit with nonessentials. This is the reason there are so many inspirational gizmos and religious knickknacks in the church today.

The human heart does not take the naked truth at its face value. It always craves truth plus some additive that will make it more palatable. The simple reason for this is that truth is seldom flattering to our human vanity. Truth tells us where we are wrong and where we need to make adjustments, and human vanity does not like that at all. Truth is a hard taskmaster and will have the whole man or none. Because of our aversion to truth, we have bought into the old song that says, "A teaspoon of sugar helps the medicine go down."

This is the problem with truth and human vanity. Human vanity wants to negotiate and keep some pet nicety, whereas truth insists on dealing with every aspect. Nobody likes to find out there is some part of his or her life or thinking that is not correct, but truth is brutal to any inconsistencies.

The average man would rather live in a golden haze of fancy than in the frozen peaks of truth. It is easier for human vanity to believe an attractive lie than to accept the harsh truth. This has made the work of deception rather easy, as a result of which the heretics are having a field day.

"Except a man be born again," Jesus taught, "he cannot see the kingdom of God" (John 3:3). That blindness makes it easy to impose on man ideas and patterns of thinking that contradict solid Bible truth. This is nowhere more dangerous than in the area of religion. Malignant spirits of evil condemn men and women, body and soul, by giving to them false faith. This has been the arsenal of the cults down through the years.

My primary concern, however, has to do with evangelical Christians. In our eagerness to reach men and women for Christ, we have sought to make truth palatable for the natural man. Not wanting to offend anybody, nor to appear judgmental, we try to make Bible truth fit the culture around us.

## A Matter of Trust

One of life's essentials is trust. Everything else builds upon this foundational concept of trust. It shapes who we are by determining our scale of values and our course in life. Where you place your trust determines, to a great extent, the quality of your life.

Some put their trust in finances. They derive a great deal of peace and contentment from piling up large storehouses of riches. Like the miser who took comfort in counting his money each evening, so do many people today find a great deal of pseudo-comfort by putting their trust in finances.

Others put their trust in their education and their ability to do things. Nothing is more satisfying to a person than the accomplishment of something significant. When a person trusts in his ability to do something, whatever that something may be, he enjoys a great deal of satisfaction—at least for a time.

I could give a long list of illustrations of how what we put our trust in brings us a certain degree of comfort and satisfaction, but I think the point is clear. The things in which we put our trust give us peace, whether that trust is based on truth or lies. If our trust is based upon a lie, it will go as far as that lie will go. Once the lie is discovered, the trust collapses.

Tell me where your trust is rooted, and I can pretty accurately describe your life. Your life cannot go any further than your trust. It is like a foundation. The foundation determines how big the building can be. If someone tries to construct a building that exceeds the potential of the foundation, there will be a collapse in the future.

So your trust is based upon either the truth or a lie. Unfortunately, the vast majority of people have placed their trust in something that has turned out to be a lie. They had every intention of believing that what they were trusting in was the absolute truth, but it turned out to be otherwise.

I want to label this the lethal lie. By that, I mean it is a lie designed deliberately by the enemy of man's soul to destroy those who believe it. It is of such a nature that it leads any person who puts their trust in it away from God and His grace. As Christians, we have an obligation to find this lethal lie and tear it apart. The only effective way to do so is to present the truth. The best way to prove that a stick is crooked is to lay a straight one beside it. No words need to be spoken.

## Lethal Lies

Let me enumerate some of the lies that men and women have trusted. They trusted these things to be true because credible men and women told them they were true. Maybe it was a minister, a Sunday School teacher or a grandparent. Even though the person passing on the lie may have had the best intentions, the lie has only one destination—and that is destruction.

The first lie I would point out is the one that says you can love the world and still be saved.

Samson was ensnared by this lie. He knew he was called of God for a particular purpose in the plan of God. He was not averse to doing God's work, but he also wanted to dabble in the pleasures of the world. The Lord said no Israelite was to have anything to do with the Philistines. Yet, Samson looked with romantic eyes across the theological fence and lusted after a Philistine woman.

Samson believed he could do God's work and also enjoy the accoutrements of the world. Many believe that today—that if they are good people, at least in their own eyes, God will understand and accept that. After all, we are told, nobody is perfect. Yet there is One who is perfect. That is the Lord Jesus Christ—and we are admonished in the Scriptures to have His mind in us. In the final judgment, we will be compared to Him.

Another lie that seems to continue unabated is that there is no hell. The people who are convinced that there is no hell are often the same ones who congratulate Jesus for being such a great teacher. Something is wrong here. Jesus, more than anyone else in Scripture, taught that there is a hell. It is inconsistent to call Him a good teacher and yet not believe that what He taught was true.

The lie about hell has been made popular by constant repetition. If you say something often enough, people will begin to believe it. Most people are not interested in proof of the authenticity of something like this. If the right person tells them something, they are going to accept it and believe it and trust it. In our culture, celebrities trump godly theologians, and what they say is believed.

Jesus is accepted as an authority on so many things—God's love and heaven, for example—but He is not considered an authority on something else He taught: hell. If what Jesus said about those other things is true, why should His teaching about hell not be believed?

I grant that it is not popular to talk about hell. Yet, if it is true—and Jesus taught that it was—it needs to be taught. The popular idea that a God of love would not send anybody to hell has no scriptural framework to support it.

Another lie is going around: There will be time after death to repent. You can live your life any which way you please. God understands that nobody is perfect, and after we die, we will have an opportunity in some purgatory somewhere to repent. The Scriptures, however, teach something altogether different. Let me repeat here that every lie of the enemy is designed to point us away from God's truth and to damn our souls.

The writer of the book of Hebrews makes it quite plain: "It is appointed unto men once to die, but after this the judgment" (Heb. 9:27). There is no time for repentance after death; rather, there is judgment. The lie that tells me I have plenty of time, and I need not worry, is a lie born in the very pit of hell itself.

Another popular lie is that our good deeds will save us. If I challenge this, some people would accuse me of being against good works. I am not. I think we ought to do as many good works as we possibly can. Our Lord, when He was on earth, went about doing good, and so should we. But the purpose of good works is not to change us, let alone save us; it is a demonstration of the change within us. No deed can change our biological status. No deed has power whatsoever to change us on the inside. A man is still flesh, though he has done good deeds all his life.

The apostle Paul writes of this:

> What shall we say then that Abraham our father, as pertaining to the flesh, hath found? For if Abraham were justified by works, he hath whereof to glory; but not before God. For what saith the scripture? Abraham believed God, and it was counted unto him for righteousness. Now to him that worketh is the reward not reckoned of grace, but of debt. But to him that worketh not, but believeth on him that justifieth the ungodly, his faith is counted for righteousness (Rom. 4:1-5).

Another lie that goes quite unchallenged is that God is too kind to punish. This brings into question God's laws. What are they for? Will God ignore His own laws? What is the purpose of God establishing laws?

This lie suggests that God will put aside laws that He has created from the foundation of the world and let people do as they please without any consequence. If I believe I can do whatever I please, I do not have to look to some higher authority. I do my own thing, and God will respect that because He is too kind to inflict punishment on me, regardless of how I have disregarded His laws.

On the other extreme, some mistakenly believe that ordinances will save. If we can just keep the ordinances and the rituals then we will be all right. I hasten to point out that one's nature cannot be changed by an ordinance. Baptizing a goat will not make him a sheep. Say a man has lived a wicked life and now comes to the point of death. The big lie perpetuated is that if some religious leader performs the right ordinance or ritual over him, he will be all right. At the very last moment, this wicked man took communion, or had the last rites said over him, so he is all right.

My question is this: *If it can change him at the end of his life, why can't it change him in the beginning?* If these rites are so powerful, you should be able to take a very wicked man, at any time in his life, have him baptized, served communion, and put through all of the religious rites available, and see him dramatically changed into a good and righteous man. It just does not happen that way.

One more lie in this category—and this is perhaps the most damaging—is that knowledge of the Bible is sufficient. If I just know what the Bible teaches, I am all right. If I have learned all the Bible stories in Sunday School, that knowledge will be sufficient for me for the rest of my life.

However, it is one thing to know about the Bible, and it is another thing to have the Bible dramatically transform your life and thinking. The Bible is the truth upon which we can base our trust. All other things are lies and will not be sufficient for our days.

The key to overcoming the lies of the enemy is not simply knowing about the Bible; it is knowing the living Word, which is none other than the Lord Jesus Christ. Remember, the hymn writer said, "Beyond the sacred page, I seek Thee, Lord." The Bible is not a piece of literature to enjoy, then close and put away until the next session. The Bible brings us face to face with Jesus.

The question comes down to this: *Upon what do you base your trust?*

The only valid trust is that which is built upon "thus saith the Lord." The human mind is easily deceived, but the heart quickened to the new birth bases its trust on the living Word, which leaves no room for deception. The Word of God is the solid foundation upon which we can stand as we battle all the lethal lies of the enemy—and as we build our lives upon this foundation of truth, we will find ourselves securely anchored upon the "Rock of Ages."

## God the Omnipotent
### Henry F. Chorley (1808–1872)
### and John Ellerton (1826–1893)

God the Omnipotent! King who ordainest
Thunder Thy clarion, the lightning Thy sword,
Show forth Thy pity on high where Thou reignest,
Give to us peace in our time, O Lord.

God the All-merciful! Earth hath forsaken
Meekness and mercy and slighted Thy word,
Let not Thy wrath in its terrors awaken,
Give to us peace in our time, O Lord.

God the All-righteous One! Man hath defied Thee,
Yet to eternity standeth Thy word,
Falsehood and wrong shall not tarry beside Thee,
Give to us peace in our time, O Lord.

So shall Thy people, with thankful devotion,
Praise Him who saved them from peril and sword;
Singing in chorus from ocean to ocean,
Peace to the nations, and praise to the Lord.
Amen.

# 10

# GOD'S FAITHFUL REBUKE TO HIS COVENANT PEOPLE

*O God, I pray that Thou wouldst stir up my heart and not
let me tolerate that which is offensive to Thee. I have grown
accustomed to my shallowness; rebuke me, O God, and turn
me from my wicked ways so that my life will be pleasing unto Thee.
I care not about pleasing the world around me, only the
Christ within me. I surrender myself to the scrutiny of Thy blessed
Word and embrace Thy judgments that will keep me walking in the
straight and narrow. In Jesus' name. Amen.*

Malachi, prophesying just after Israel had returned from exile,
called his message to God's people: "The burden of the word of
the LORD to Israel by Malachi" (Mal. 1:1). That exile had been a
judgment for their sin, and now the people were knee-deep in
sin again. Malachi's word to them had to be a "burden." I am
sure that as he uttered these words, his heart was breaking
within him for the condition of his own people.

The condition of Israel at that time mirrors the condition
of Christianity in general today. We can boast about our past

deliverances. We can celebrate our "freedom in Christ." But we face the identical condition that necessitated divine deliverance for our forefathers: We celebrate the victory while forgetting the long and heartbreaking path that led to that victory.

As one examines history, one of the bitterest conclusions one must draw in the area of religion is that history teaches us nothing except that it does not teach us anything. The present generation has not learned from the past generation, and it is unlikely that the future generation will learn from the present generation. This is a sad commentary on a generation that has more research technology and resources available to it than any previous generation. There is not a fact or event in history that someone today cannot read about. It must be exasperating to God, to put it in human terms, to see His people in such a circle of repetition.

Many put great value on experience—but experiences are valueless unless we absolutely surrender to God. In fact, I might say that nothing has any value until we have come to that ultimate point of surrendering ourselves to God. It is out of our surrender that God can begin to use us and bless us. Until we surrender, our value is quite questionable.

What good is experience if it does not lead us to God? There is potential for great tragedy here. Think of the tragedy of wasted suffering. A person endures terrible suffering and comes out on the other side empty and valueless. The same can be true with pain. What good is it to go through a painful experience and not be any better for it?

We sometimes evaluate experience by what a person has gone through, but God values experience insomuch as it brings us to Him. I must point out right here that many times religion comes between our experience and our encounter with God. Whatever the cause may be, any experience that does not include or end with a personal encounter with God carries with it no value.

Many times a person will go through an experience, lose everything, and then have to start all over again, unchanged from before.

The victory is only truly a victory when it enables us to conquer that which brought us down in the first place. The person may recover from some tragedy, but if all they do is start over again, they are doomed to repeat the tragedy *ad nauseam*.

## What Does It Mean to Be a "Covenant People"?

As Christians, we put a lot of stock in the idea of a covenant. God has established a covenant with us. We like to think of ourselves as a covenant people. We have a relationship with God that cannot be broken by anything or anyone less than God. Understandably, we find a great deal of comfort, satisfaction and security in this covenant relationship.

What is often overlooked in this covenant relationship is that God will not leave a covenant people long unreproved. Within a covenant relationship, the interactions are not all positive. Thank God for the positive elements associated with my covenant relationship with Him! But along with those positive elements are some negative ones that are often overlooked by the present generation of Christians.

Yes, God encourages us, blesses us, and provides for us richly. However, God is not a God who closes His eyes to the dangers facing His covenant people—including those dangers that stem from our own behavior. He rebukes us in the present so that we may escape His judgment in the end. Those whom He does not rebuke now will ultimately face the wrath of His judgment.

Because I am in a covenant relationship with God, I am under His review—which is the most loving thing our heavenly Father can do for us. "Whom the Lord loveth he chasteneth" (Heb. 12:6).

When a large-scale tragedy happens in the world around us, many people immediately assume that God is judging the non-believing world. There is some truth in this, but I would remind you of what the Scripture says. The Bible tells us that judgment begins in the house of God. God deals with His covenant people first. The kindest act of God may be to rebuke us and turn us from the tragedy of sin.

It is natural for us to look for consolation, even when we have earned judgment. Some people say that all they want is what they deserve. I certainly do not want what I deserve. I know that, on my own, all I deserve is hell. It is the kindness of God that rebukes me in such a way as to turn me away from the path that leads to hellfire and damnation. I do not want what I deserve; I want to throw myself on the mercy of God. The most gracious aspect of God's mercy is His faithfulness in rebuking my wayward ways.

Because I am part of God's covenant people, I come under His warning, His rebuke, and the shocking exposure of unsuspected wickedness. God leaves no stone unturned in His pursuit of our holiness. God is busy in my life, rooting out everything that is offensive to Him. To ignore God's rebukes and try to sneak into His comfort is folly. God cannot accept sin in any degree. Those things in us that are contrary to His holy nature will, under His gracious attention, be rebuked and judged.

All through Christendom, we boast of our covenant relationship. We look hungrily for the assurance that we are all right, but the truth of the matter is that we have sinned against revealed light. That is the tragedy of our situation—not so much that we are stumbling around in darkness, but that we are doing so when we are meant to be children of the light. The atrocity of our situation is that we are rebelling against God's light.

## Judgment in Our Generation

In the Church in America today, we have tolerated injustice and crime through weakness. We tolerate sin by excusing it and even making light of it. Every unpunished murder in our country must be punished in blood. Every injustice must be overturned. God's justice demands this.

We sometimes believe that America is an upright and righteous nation. All anybody has to do to challenge this notion is look around and see our culture and society through the binoculars of God's Word. If what we see out in the world does not harmonize with what we see in the Word, we are headed for judgment. This judgment, as I mentioned, begins in the house of the Lord.

If we look into the church and the doings of the church in contemporary society, and then compare what we see there with what we see in the Living Word of God and find any inconsistencies, then judgment must come. The choice is then ours. We can judge ourselves and deal with the iniquities within our fellowship, or God will send the judgment on us. I certainly do not want to judge anybody, but it seems to me that much of American Christianity is under the judgment of God.

The ominous sign of this is that our leaders show no disposition to be sorry for sin. Regularly we hear about sin in the church, especially among top-level church leaders, and for the most part, it is not judged or condemned; rather, it is excused. Nobody seems to be sorry for their sin. They may be sorry that they were caught, but that does not lead to a change of life.

It is easy to find sin in the other person—to point at somebody else and condemn his or her sin. But our evaluation needs to begin with ourselves: *What in me needs to be rebuked by the Word of God?* There seems to be plenty of blame to go around, but I find very little penitence.

All around our world, we can see that God's judgments are on the earth. War is God's scourge over the nations today. Where can you find an area of the globe not suffering from this? One area quiets down only for other areas to flare up in anger and break out into war. This is the fate that befalls a world in rebellion against God. Where there is no peace in the heart, there will be no peace on the earth. Only the Prince of Peace can bring to our world the kind of peace that will eliminate everything that feeds into a war culture.

I believe we are living in a generation that is un-rebuked. There was a time, not so long ago, when even out in the world there was a check on sin. There were certain things that shamed individuals, our communities and our nation. Have we come to the point in this generation where we no longer can be shamed by anything?

Sin has become a joke that comedians cash in on in the hellholes called nightclubs. Debauchery is the vogue of the day. Tolerance of this has enlarged with each generation, to the point that this generation seems not to be embarrassed by anything.

This generation is among the most un-chastised, arrogant and presumptuous people. Everyone does that which is right in his own eyes. Do what pleases you regardless of who else it displeases. It is the "me" generation.

## The Role of God's Covenant People

All of what I have just described is going on around those who call themselves the covenant people of God. Has the Church of

Jesus Christ lost its influence in the world? Are we no longer a rebuke to the sinful ways of the culture?

There is a new church today—a new brand of Christianity that is running rampant. This new church is seeking assurance by adding up her virtues. "Look at me," she says with an arrogant spirit. Never in our country have we seen bigger church buildings or larger congregations. Never has there been more social activity than there is today. For the most part, we take courage from numbers. "That must be a good church—look at all of the people going there," is the reasoning one hears today.

We have fallen into the gutter of the numbers game. For my part, I would rather be associated with a small body of believers who are living a life of holiness—constantly being rebuked by God and dealing with sin day by day—than be part of a huge group of people who are satisfied in their self-assurance and take comfort in the idea that God must be on their side because they are prosperous.

Prosperity is not the sign of the covenant people of God. The sign of the covenant people of God is that they own up to their sin and forsake it; they experience the rebuke of God and turn from a pathway leading to destruction. We should turn away from our sin and walk a path of holiness—a path of which the Scripture says, "Narrow is the way" (Matt. 7:14). The Christian ideology being practiced today has so broadened the way that it is impossible for anybody to go to hell.

What needs to be done?

We dare not trust in our glorious past. Many like to point to the past and take comfort in the fact that it is their heritage and legacy. I point out that if what took place in the past is not replicated in the present, then it is of no effect to us. The past dies with those who composed it. We cannot live in the past or the shadow of its greatness.

We dare not look towards a glorious future unless we are willing to create a glorious present. To do that means bringing ourselves, as the covenant people of God, under the review and judgment of God now. It means taking care of our situation and allowing God to do what He desires to do in us and through us. Let us not wait until Judgment Day. Let that Judgment Day be now. Allow the Word of the living God to rebuke us the same way we allow it to encourage us.

The burden of the Word of the Lord is simply for those of us who are the covenant people of God to bring ourselves under the jurisdiction, both positive and negative, of the Scriptures. As we do that, we will begin to live daily in the power of the Holy Spirit as the Word of God becomes a reality in us.

When my friend Tom Haire was leaving America to go back to his home in Ireland, I asked if he was going to go back and do a lot of preaching. "No," Tom said thoughtfully, "I'm going to go back and spend the next few months judging myself while I still have time to do something about it."

Now is the time to judge ourselves and allow the Holy Spirit to point out the iniquities in our life—so that we have time to make those things right. Nothing seems more important to me than balancing the books of my life while I still have the opportunity to do something about any errors I may find in the course of self-examination.

## May the Mind of Christ, My Savior
### Kate Barclay Wilkinson (1859–1928)

May the mind of Christ, my Savior,
Live in me from day to day,
By His love and power controlling
All I do and say.

May the Word of God dwell richly
In my heart from hour to hour,
So that all may see I triumph
Only through His power.

May the peace of God my Father
Rule my life in everything,
That I may be calm to comfort
Sick and sorrowing.

May the love of Jesus fill me
As the waters fill the sea;
Him exalting, self abasing,
This is victory.

May I run the race before me,
Strong and brave to face the foe,
Looking only unto Jesus
As I onward go.

May His beauty rest upon me,
As I seek the lost to win,
And may they forget the channel,
Seeing only Him.

# 11

# Dealing with the Assault to God's Power

*The power of Thy kingdom, O God, is not in words only, but in the power and demonstration of the Holy Spirit. May my life go beyond the mere utterance of words, and may I experience the power of the Holy Spirit transforming me into that which will please Thee. This I ask in Jesus' name. Amen.*

One of the greatest arguments within the church is in the area of power. There are many power-hungry people in the church today, but this is not something new. In the apostle Paul's day, many were willing to challenge his authority and more than willing to push him out of the way in order to advance their own authority.

Solomon in all his wisdom was right: "The thing that hath been, it is that which shall be; and that which is done is that which shall be done: and there is no new thing under the sun" (Eccles. 1:9).

Paul, the apostle, received his authority directly from Christ. Although vigorously contested in his day, it was nevertheless authority from Christ, who is the true head of the Church. Paul was appointed by the Lord to exercise this authority in a variety of ways.

He was to receive and shape church truth. Up until this point, all Scripture had to do with Jewish law. It was Paul's responsibility to help lay the foundation that would undergird the Church of Jesus Christ. This in and of itself was a horrific responsibility. If you do not get things right in the beginning, plenty of problems will ensue in the future.

Many of the epistles Paul wrote had to do with this shaping of church truth and policy. He was laying down the framework upon which the ministry of the Church would be built. Of course, the true Foundation and chief Cornerstone is none other than the Lord Jesus Christ. Some would build the Church upon Peter, but Paul, with his Christ-given commission, built the New Testament Church upon the Lord Jesus.

Part of his responsibility was to set up the system and polity for the Church to govern itself. This was no easy task. Everybody wants to have a say in the way things are supposed to go. But whatever else the New Testament Church of Jesus Christ was, it was not democratic. It was not Paul's responsibility to get everybody together and say to them, "Brethren, what do you think about this?" That is the way we often do things today, but it was not the way the apostle Paul did it—and it is not the way Christ desires His Church to operate.

Nobody understood the Church as completely as the apostle Paul did. Every generation wants to try to improve on what Paul laid down—or at least to modify and redefine it for their time. The apostle Paul had the authority to lay down the structure of the New Testament Church, and I believe we are under the obligation to adhere to that structure regardless of cultural demands. We are either a church according to the New Testament model or we are not.

Paul embodied the authority he had been given and showed by example how the Church was to work. He did not merely scribble down rules and regulations on a manuscript; rather, he displayed the principles he taught in his own life and ministry.

The problem Paul faced was the presence of those who participated in schisms within the New Testament Church. As these individuals could not carry on as they wanted to under Paul's authority, they made it their mission to repudiate his teaching and to do everything within their power to undermine and destroy his authority.

The community of believers in Corinth was especially threatened by such divisive behavior. Paul sent Timothy to plead his cause to the church there. Timothy represented Paul—presenting the church with Paul's credentials, if you will. Paul finally had to warn the Corinthian Christians that his authority did not rest in human eloquence or speech, but rather in the power entrusted to him by the Head of the Church, the Lord Jesus Christ.

## Not in Words, but in Power

In dealing with this issue, the apostle Paul articulated a very important truth: The kingdom is not in words only, but in power (see 1 Cor. 4:20). To understand this difference is to understand the power and authority of the Church of Jesus Christ. The problem with those involved in the schisms was that they did not understand this difference. They assumed that the words themselves held the power; therefore, if they used the words, they had the power.

I think that this is a major problem in the evangelical church today. We are caught up with words and phrases, striving to update our religious vocabulary to harmonize with the culture around us. We think that if we use words people understand, they will get the power. Synchronize all you please with the world around you, but the power of God is not in human eloquence or reason. It is wholly in the work of the Holy Spirit through the living Word.

In thinking about this, one must understand that it takes words to form truth. You cannot have truth expressed apart from words. But while words are the form of truth, they are the outward image only. This is where we generally make our mistake. The words only represent the power that is in the Word.

Our words can never be the inner essence, but only the outer shell; they are incidental, and can never be fundamental. Words are slippery—we see this sometimes in Bible translations. One version translates a certain Greek word one way, while another version translates it a different way. It is the same Greek word, but there are nuances of meaning that can sometimes affect the truth.

What we sometimes fail to understand is that there is an essence of truth. All truth begins with God; therefore, it is very hard to boil it down to a word or a phrase. Truth follows the form of words, but it sometimes deserts that form and goes beyond.

Many illustrations could be used here, but allow me an obvious one. When one person uses the word "love," he may mean something different from when someone else uses the same word. In fact, about four Greek words can be translated "love."

When a father says to his son, "I love you," it means something different from when that son meets a young girl of his dreams and says to her, "I love you." They use the same words, and yet the ramification of the meaning is quite different. That is a rather silly illustration, but it reminds us that we need to be careful that we are not limiting spiritual truths to a set of words or phrases.

The great error of our day is holding the form to be the essence. We think we can sum up the kingdom of God in words. We are not alone in this fallacy; this seems to have been the great error since the days of the New Testament Church. What the apostle Paul tried to get the Christians of his day to understand is that you cannot boil the Church down to phrases and words. Words can deceive and can be misleading.

Some believe there is safety in mumbling words. It does not matter if you really understand what those words mean; if you utter them repeatedly, it will bring some sort of comfort and safety to your heart.

Others would have you believe there is power in certain words to fight off Satan. If you just have the right words—the right formula—you can back the devil into a corner. No matter what you say, if you end it with "in Jesus' name," it will be done—God does not have any choice in the matter. How utterly foolish! No demon in hell fears words alone. It is only when those words serve as a channel through which the power of God flows that they have potency.

Some believe that there is power in words to bring good. This is the error of positive thinking. Just think positive thoughts and say positive words—and everything will turn out all right. It is possible, so these would have you believe, to think your way out of any and every problem; all you need to do is fill your head with the right thoughts.

The apostle Paul seeks to convince the Corinthian church that the kingdom of Jesus Christ does not lie in mere words. The kingdom of God, according to Paul, is in power. Its essence is in power. This power is the Holy Spirit operating through the Word. It is the power of the risen Christ manifested by the Holy Spirit in the Church of Jesus Christ. Not only words, but also the manifestation of the Holy Spirit.

There is absolutely no way you can boil the Holy Spirit down to mere words or a simple formula. There is power associated with the work of the Holy Spirit in conjunction with the Scriptures that goes beyond the words on the page. No matter how beautiful or how realistic a painting of a fire might be, it will never warm anyone.

Paul's challenge to those who created schisms in the church was that when he came, they could demonstrate their words, and he would demonstrate his power. His power was in the Holy Spirit manifesting in his life through the Scriptures. We cannot get away from this. There are those who have a power agenda for themselves. They want people to believe they possess power—if they speak it, it will be so.

Paul tells us that the power associated with the New Testament Church is that which comes by the Holy Spirit manifesting through the Word of God. You cannot take the two and separate them. It is not the Holy Spirit alone, and it is not the Word of God alone; it is the two in harmonious unity.

Here is where the Church is divided. On one hand are those who emphasize the power of the Holy Spirit to the exclusion of everything else, including the Bible. They would have the Holy Spirit do things contrary to the plain teaching of the Word of God. On the other hand, we see those who emphasize the Word of God to the exclusion of everything else, even the Holy Spirit. If you have the words, so they believe, you have everything you need. "I claim it, therefore it is mine."

Paul made it clear that the Kingdom does not come in word only, but in power. There is cooperation between the Holy Spirit and the Word of God—a cooperation that cannot be denied without doing harm to the New Testament Church. The Holy Spirit does nothing apart from or contrary to the Word of God.

What are the workings of this power that Paul is talking about?

## The Workings of God's Power

First, it is a moral power. By that, I mean that its purpose is to expose sin to the sinner's heart. The power of the Word of God is to show me where I am wrong. It does not stop there, however; it also works to revolutionize and convert me into the image of Christ. The moral power Paul is talking about creates holy men and women who will manifest the nature of Christ to a fallen world.

It is also a persuasive power. It convinces, persuades, and breaks down all resistance to the will of God. It is a power that goes beyond mere words—and it is a power that words cannot stand up against.

Let us recall David's slaying of Goliath. From a human standpoint, Goliath had the day. Everything was on his side. But because David was working under the power and authority of Jehovah, it became Jehovah's day. As well armored as Goliath was, he was no match for this little boy with the slingshot who had behind him the power of Jehovah. God wields a persuasive power that nothing in this world can stand against.

I also believe it is a worship power. Worship has been given a bad connotation in our generation. Many things pass for worship that the apostle Paul would be most infuriated about and vehemently speak out against. The power of worship is to create reverence. This is lacking in today's evangelical church. Some Sunday worship services are nothing more than a slightly religious hootenanny. There is no sense of reverence—no awe at being in the presence of God. You cannot talk anybody into reverence. It is the power of worship that brings us into this state.

I believe the power of worship is also to excite ecstasy—to lift us above the common and normal into the rarefied air of worship and adoration and praise—a place where no flesh can venture unaided. Where is the ecstasy in our worship services today? Where is the wonder? Where is the silence before God's awful manifested presence?

This power is also a magnetic power. By that, I mean that it draws us to Christ. It will exalt Him above all things. You will know that it is the power of God when Jesus Christ is exalted above all other things. When there is the exaltation of the personality or the celebrity, you can be sure it is not the power of the Holy Spirit at work. This magnetic power cannot be replicated by mere words. Jesus said, "And I, if I be lifted up from the earth, will draw all men unto me" (John 12:32).

## The Task for the Church Today

Paul made his case to the Corinthian church. He faced up to those who created schisms not in words only but also in the power and demonstration of the Holy Spirit. As he laid the foundation for the New Testament Church—of which we are part—he demanded no deviation from these central truths.

I think we must make certain demands in the evangelical church today. We must demand that we have more than just correct doctrine. Having correct doctrine is important, but it is not sufficient. A person can believe the right things and still not be right with God. A person can know all of the right words, and still never have been changed inwardly. This is the difference between information and transformation.

We also need to demand more than just right living. Many people can live right. Many cults have a strict demand that their followers live right. Some cult members live lives more blameless than believers. We are meant for more than just right living; Christ offers us life flowing from the inner witness of the Holy Spirit.

We also need to demand that our church be more than just friendly. Sure, it is important to be friendly. When people visit our church, we should greet them with a smile and welcome them. The church, however, is about more than just being friendly—or being loyal, or being united on certain issues. These are all surface matters and do not get to the heart or core of true spiritual fellowship. All of these can be accomplished in human strength.

How can we become the people and the Church whom we are meant to be? How can we transition from mere words into the power and demonstration of the Holy Spirit? Let me suggest three disciplines.

First, there is prayer. We must give ourselves to prayer that goes beyond just the mumbling of certain words. I believe all prayer begins with words—but it does not end there. There comes a time when our prayer transitions to something other than mere words, and we come into the *Mysterium Tremendum* of God's presence. I am speaking of that reverential awe of entering into His manifest presence and basking in the sunlight of His pleasure. We have not truly prayed until we have broken through the mystic veil and entered the manifested presence of the One to whom we are praying.

Then there is faith. Faith is more than just believing the right words. "Faith cometh by hearing," the apostle Paul said, "and hearing by the word of God" (Rom. 10:17). I believe it is impossible to boil my faith down to a series of words. My faith rises above words and rests in the very heart of God. My trust is in God—not in my explanation of who God is. If what I believe in can be explained, it is not God.

The last discipline is surrender. Surrender is not just something we talk about; rather, it is something we have to do. We cannot surrender in word; we must surrender in deed. If we are going to build our life upon the foundation the apostle Paul established for the New Testament Church, we will have to surrender our ideas, our understanding and our explanations, and accept Jesus Christ for who He really is—the living Word.

## Once For All
### Philip P. Bliss (1838–1876)

Free from the law, O happy condition,
Jesus has bled and there is remission,
Cursed by the law and bruised by the fall,
Grace hath redeemed us once for all.

Now we are free, there's no condemnation,
Jesus provides a perfect salvation.
"Come unto Me," O hear His sweet call,
Come, and He saves us once for all.

Children of God, O glorious calling,
Surely His grace will keep us from falling;
Passing from death to life at His call;
Blessed salvation once for all.

Once for all, O sinner, receive it,
Once for all, O brother, believe it;
Cling to the cross, the burden will fall,
Christ hath redeemed us once for all.

# 12

# THE EFFECT OF GOD'S WORD IN A PERSON'S LIFE

*Thy Word, O God, has been my portion each day. I did eat
and it did nourish my spirit. Its sweetness enticed me to endure
the bitterness of following Thee in a world contrary to Thee and
Thy holiness. My spirit hungers for Thee; nothing else fully satisfies.
I pledge before Thee that I will not sing a song I am not willing
to live. It is my pleasure, O Christ, to identify with Thee and
the curse of Thy cross. Amen.*

The Old Testament prophet Ezekiel testified, "And he said
unto me, Son of man, cause thy belly to eat, and fill thy bowels
with this roll that I give thee. Then did I eat it; and it was in my
mouth as honey for sweetness" (Ezek. 3:3).

Over in the New Testament, in the book of Revelation, we
find this: "And I went unto the angel, and said unto him, Give
me the little book. And he said unto me, Take it, and eat it up;
and it shall make thy belly bitter, but it shall be in thy mouth
sweet as honey" (Rev. 10:9).

There is a cause and effect relationship between the eating
of the book and the result of bitterness in the belly. When the
Word of the Lord is digested—that is, when it gets down into a

person and becomes part of his life, and when it dictates the witness of the Christian or gives the prophet his message—it becomes bitter. It becomes bitter to the flesh because of the hostile attitude of the world, the weakness of the flesh, and the sinister hatred of the devil. The Word of God is sweet to the taste and strong to deliver, but it also has a way of getting a people who live by it into trouble.

## A Major Disaster

The human race is in a bad way—although you will find many men who will say otherwise, telling us what a wonderful bunch we are and even writing books on the subject. Occasionally, I get letters advising me not to take such a dark view of the world, because, after all, the world is good, if we only could look on the bright side. This is bad advice.

There is in the world a major disaster; it has come about by the fall of man. The sin of man has brought an alienation from God. That is, it has broken off relationship with God, and it has brought that which we call mortality—which, of course, is that we are subject to die—and it has brought death itself. We must watch lest when we are looking over the human race and see how they suffer—how there is death and mortality and disease and insanity and crime and all these things—we become sentimental about it and begin to pity people instead of realizing that we are to blame.

Some say that sin is a disease, something like polio. You get it, you cannot help having it, and it kills you, but you are not to blame for it. You are a poor fellow and have no more responsibility for your illness than does a child who is born with a bad heart. You cannot help it; you were born into the world that way.

Our Lord told us about a prodigal, the younger of two brothers, who went out into the world deliberately, engaged in riotous living deliberately, spent all that he had deliberately, and was reduced to poverty and rags, as a result of which he was forced to work in the field, laboring for swine keepers. All of this was his own fault. It was not the result of something he could not help, as polio or a heart attack might be. It was his own doing. The human race is in a bad way, but we are in a bad way by our own fault.

## Saved, but Not Rescued

We have been redeemed through the atonement made by Jesus Christ our Lord on the cross. Through this act of propitiation for our sins, we who are Christians have justification and regeneration. We are justified, that is declared righteous before God; we are regenerated, that is born a second time. We have all this, but we are not rescued.

Whenever there has been a revival, the Church always begins by acknowledging and making a part of her very lifeblood the belief that we are in a bad fix, that there has been a major disaster, and that while through the Christian faith, God saves, we are not yet rescued. We live in peril; we are sheep in the midst of wolves. You will find this truth set forth in Paul's epistles:

For the earnest expectation of the creature waiteth for the manifestation of the sons of God. For the creature was made subject to vanity, not willingly, but by reason of him who hath subjected the same in hope. Because the creature itself [that is, creation] also shall be delivered from the bondage of corruption into the glorious liberty of the children of God. For we know that the whole creation groaneth and travaileth in pain together until now. And not only they, but ourselves also, which have the firstfruits of the Spirit, even we ourselves groan within ourselves, waiting for the adoption, to wit, the redemption of our body (Rom. 8:19-23).

In 2 Corinthians, the eleventh chapter, Paul gives a long list of troubles he had faced—imprisonment, beatings, shipwrecks, and so forth. He was saved, but, according to his testimony, he was not yet rescued. He was redeemed, but not yet out of the fire. That is exactly where the Church finds herself today.

The true Church of Christ is a redeemed Church—born of the Spirit and washed in the blood, with her judgments behind her—but she is not yet rescued. She has her name written in heaven, but she is on earth—and as long as she is on earth, and acting like the Church, she is going to be in trouble. Now, if she stops acting like the Church, she will not have troubles anymore—except, of course, those troubles which come to all men alike.

This is truth you do not often hear taught, but we are asked to eat the truth, just as the prophets were. In fact, we are ordered to eat the truth—to take the book into our system until it permeates every part of us. In the blunt Elizabethan days, they did not hesitate to say until it goes down through your belly and into your digestive system; until it permeates every part of your life to the extent that there is no antidote for it and no escape from it; until there is total commitment, and the truth takes full control, and the cross becomes an instinct.

Truth is always very sweet at first. When we sing truth, it is very sweet. When we read it, it is very sweet. But when it takes over—when it begins to control us and determine our lives, and becomes to us a reflex, a second nature, a mastery impulse—

then it becomes as bitter as gall to the carnal nature, because truth has consequences.

If we were in heaven, truth would be uniformly sweet. Nobody would ever complain about the bitterness of truth if we were all in heaven. However, we are not in heaven, but halfway between heaven and hell—we are here in this world. We are not in hell, and thank God, we are not going to be. We are not in heaven, but, praise God, we are going to be. No, we are halfway between heaven and hell, in this world of good and bad—this world of saints and sinners, of joy and sorrow—and so truth sometimes is very harsh.

Our difficulty is that we, even God's people, do not allow the truth to get down into our system. It is sharp, and we do not like its sharpness. It is painful, and we do not like its painfulness. It is bitter, and we do not like its bitterness. Therefore, we compromise.

How many are really eating the book? I know we memorize it in Sunday School; we read it through in a year, read our chapter each day, study the Sunday School lesson, and may even teach. However, I wonder how many of us have eaten it and let it get down into our system until there is no antidote for it? Most people prefer to pray with their fingers crossed; they are ready to start following the Lord with the understanding that if things get tough, they are going to go back.

We get on our knees and say, "Oh God, take all of me—but not quite." "Oh God, make me a holy man—but not altogether so." "Oh God, take everything I have—but not quite everything I have." We are always putting in this proviso: "Lord, this is off if I get in a tight spot."

We have made a crucial error in our understanding. We think that because we have been redeemed, we have been rescued. But this is not the case. We are kept by the power of God through faith unto salvation, ready to be revealed in the last time. Our salvation is sure enough, but we have not yet been rescued.

The battle is still on. The fight is still here. The enemy is still around us. We are still grasshoppers in the wilderness. We are still sheep in the desert. We are still children, wandering through the earth. We are still good people in a bad world—a world that will crush us and destroy us if it can.

This is one of the most ominous things I see in modern Christianity; we want to use the cross to save us from the cross. We cannot use the cross to save ourselves from the cross. The cross—that is, Jesus our Lord dying on the cross and rising again—will save us, but that same cross has to do something in us and to us and for us—and, frankly, some will not have it. When we believe in Christ, we like for it to mean that we join a pleasant fellowship, form regular religious habits, quit the dirtiest kinds of iniquity, go to banquets, sing choruses, and go to summer conventions.

That does not sound to me like Paul. It does not sound like the prophets, and it does not sound like the disciple John. It does not sound like Noah, or like Luther, or like Knox. It does not sound like any of them, because they did not look at a life of faith like that. They did not say, "I'm going to believe in Christ and join a pleasant fellowship and form regular religious habits, and then from hereon everything is going to be wonderful. Thereafter, I'm going to take it relatively easy. I will work for Christ, but be reasonable about it."

## Will We Swallow the Roll?

The trouble with most Christians is that they refuse to eat the roll. They nibble at it, but will not swallow it. They listen to it, but will not let it get hold of them. They are going to control it, and not the other way around. They buy a new Bible every five years and read it through—but they are not going to let the Bible control them. They will not do that, because it will make their belly bitter. It will be harsh, sharp and painful, and they will not have it. They are going to manipulate the Word instead of allowing the Word to manipulate them.

Paul said, in Romans 5, that some people would die for others; a few people would dare to do so. Some people have in fact died for somebody else. They loved them so much. I have children; as they grew up, I knew God would not have had to ask me twice—I would gladly have given my life for them. It is not all heroic on my part. I simply love my children a little more than I love myself.

I think it quite strange that when we come to Christianity, we are unwilling to commit ourselves like that. We want to find a way out—a way back to the life we had before. We want to find a parenthesis somewhere that we can duck into to save going through the whole scene. We want in some way to get around this idea of total commitment.

I would not hesitate to say this: All over the North American continent, from Key West to the farthest point north in Canada, and from the Atlantic to the Pacific, I believe there are evangelical Christians who believe all right and nibble the Word, but are not committed to a point where their economic interests are going to be jeopardized. They are going to look after their economic interests first, and they have somehow or other managed to compromise themselves before God in order to make their conscience amenable to them. They have tamed their conscience as you might tame a house cat—so that it lies down and purrs at their feet—and they have no trouble at all, because they have compromised between serving God and protecting their economic interest.

This does not mean that they do not give their tithe; it just means that they are not going to jeopardize themselves. They are not going to put themselves in a place where they may lose everything. They explain, "I don't believe God wants that." Then they go on to rationalize their statement: "If I jeopardize what I have and lose it all, I can't give to missionaries, can I?" The compromise is made, and the book is spit out—it has been chewed, but not swallowed. It is very sweet in your mouth while you are chewing it, provided you do not swallow it and allow it to get down into your system.

I wonder how many Christian businessmen would swallow the book down into their system—knowing that their economic interest might blow up in their face—for Christ's sake? I do not think there would be very many. The philosophy of a good many of my dear friends who have a great deal of money is that the Lord gave them everything they have—and because He gave it to them, it is theirs to keep.

I wonder if there are any—and if so, how many and where they are—who would allow their total commitment to Christ to jeopardize their blood ties. By this I mean, would they allow themselves to be separated from family for the sake of the gospel?

In some parts of the world, when somebody is converted, he has to say goodbye to his father and mother—and to all the taboos and ties of the tribe—and go away. In some sects, if a Jew is converted to Christ—if he really believes on Christ and knows Him as his Messiah—his family holds a funeral for him. They reckon him dead and never mention his name or communicate with him again. He turns from the mother who gave him birth and the father whose gnarled hands worked to bring him up, says goodbye to them, and walks out of the house—never to be known by them again. That is total commitment.

American evangelical Christians these days are not going to go as far as all that. We consider such behavior to be a bit fanatical and quite ridiculous. We are going to believe on Christ and join a pleasant fellowship and form some good religious habits and then take things relatively easy. We are not going to jeopardize blood ties.

A man says, "I would like to give myself to Jesus Christ, but I can't. I couldn't break up our home." A woman says, "I would give myself to Christ, but my husband would brutalize me; he wouldn't allow it." A son says, "I'd give myself to Jesus Christ, but I'd have to leave my home if I did." These did not swallow the book; they just nibbled at it.

Then I think about friendships. Friendships are beautiful things. Henry David Thoreau and Ralph Waldo Emerson, who were themselves friends, wrote essays on friendship. Emerson's concept of friendship was that your friend was somebody for whom you could do something. Thoreau's concept was that your friend was somebody who could do something for you. These are two very different ways of looking at friendship.

However you define friendship, are there many who would give up their friends for Christ's sake? What about their comforts? Are there any who would commit themselves to such a degree that they jeopardize their health for Christ's sake? Most of us do not want to jeopardize our health, although we sometimes do so for the things of the world.

A man, for instance, will drink himself drunk and lie in the gutter, or he will overeat until he is full of cholesterol. But when it comes to religion, he says, "Oh no. You don't mean I'm to be a fanatic, do you?" The fanatic is somebody who takes Jesus Christ seriously. This is some people's concept of a fanatic: somebody who believes what Jesus Christ said and follows Him wherever He goes.

Jesus was willing to jeopardize His health. When they came to Him and said, "You know what's going to happen to You, don't You? They'll kill You if You don't look out. That old man, Herod, is looking for You now," Jesus replied, "Go tell Herod, that old fox, that I'll be around a while yet. Tell him I'll still be here." He literally put not just His health but His very life in jeopardy, giving Himself to die for the unjust so that He might lead us to God.

The people of God ought to be people who have chewed the book, swallowed the book, digested the book, and absorbed the book until it has colored them and given them the right complexion. You should not be able to touch the person of God anywhere; when you stretch out your fingers toward him, you should touch only the book.

God's people are called to be heroic. They are called to ingest and work through even the difficult truths contained in God's Word. Instead, we nurse on the sweet book. What a dear book it is. What a sweet book. We run to get another translation of the sweet book, in order to get a little more flavor. We are not, however, going to let it change us very much.

## A Church in Need of Revival

Revival happens when a good percentage of the people in a church or other gathering decide to swallow the book and let it have its effect on their lives, come what may. In some solemn hour before God, they decide they are going to chew that book up, swallow it down, get it into their system, and let it take root where there cannot be an antidote for it. It is going to do its work; it is going to have its effect upon them. It will become second nature to them and their mastering impulse—and when God sees people who are like that, the Holy Ghost is poured out.

The danger we face today is this: We believe that because we are evangelical in our creed, we are therefore pleasing God, the Father Almighty. But it may be that our evangelical creed is merely nibbling the sweet book and never allowing it to get into our system where it can change our lives and make us different—where it can jeopardize our security and put a cross on our back and make us bold soldiers—and even martyrs, if need be. I wonder if God will not pass by those who have been nibbling this sweet book and go among those who have been starved for a half a century and do a wonderful miracle of grace there. Perhaps He will pour waters upon them that are thirsty and send a flood over the dry ground.

I do not charge anybody. I am afraid for my own heart and worried for myself—not about my salvation, my justification or my eternal life, but about whether I am a man so completely committed that if my income were all suddenly to be taken, I would thank God and go ahead anyhow. If my friends were all suddenly to desert me, I would look up and thank God and go ahead anyhow. If I felt my health suddenly deteriorating, I would look up and thank God and go ahead anyhow.

We need a revival, a spiritual reformation that will change everything. We need to chew the book and swallow it so that we cannot regurgitate it. We must come to the point where we have no place to hide, no way to compromise, no bridge to go back over, no excuse to offer, no compromise to make—no way to get out of our commitment to Christ.

It will make you bitter. How can one help but be bitter in a world that hates God—in a world that crucified Jesus and never repented of it? Yes, we will be bitter in a world where retailers will make untold fortunes on His birthday but would not follow Him from here to the corner. That is the kind of world we live in.

The Lord has called us to be a spiritual people, a godly people, a committed people, a worshiping people, a people for His own possession, a peculiar people. Are we willing to allow His Word to make us into all those things?

## The Sacred Book
Thomas Kelly (1769–1855)

I love the sacred book of God;
No other can its place supply;
It points me to the saints' abode,
It gives me wings, and bids me fly.

Sweet book! in thee my eyes discern
The image of my absent Lord:
From thine instructive page I learn
The joys his presence will afford.

But while I'm here, thou shalt supply
His place and tell me of his love:
I'll read with faith's discerning eye,
And thus partake of joys above.

# PART III

* * * * * * * * * * * * * * *

# RELEASING GOD'S POWER THROUGH THE WORD

*Let thy mercies come also unto me, O LORD,*
*even thy salvation, according to thy word.*

PSALM 119:41

# 13

# The Christian's Ladder of Spiritual Power

*O God, the God of everlasting truth, I come and bow before Thee.
Thy Word is my rock and foundation during weary times. I trust in
Thee and look to Thee for my daily portion of grace. Thy promises have
been true in all generations, and I rest my life upon all the unfolding
promises of Thy Word. Thy promises, like flowers in the garden, have
filled my life with the fragrance of Thy presence. Amen.*

The most amazing thing to me about the Christian life is the
growing or progressing nature of my personal relationship
with God through Jesus Christ. The overwhelming evidence
suggests that not many Christians today are experiencing this
progression, which I will call the ladder of spiritual power.
God's promises, as administered by the Holy Spirit, empower
us to increase in our ability to know God and fulfill His purposes for our lives.

I base the ladder image on the vision Jacob had one night,
early in his life, while he was running away from a brother he
had tricked out of some inheritance and the father he had lied
to. That night, Jacob so encountered the Lord as to change his
entire concept of God. We refer to this as Jacob's ladder.

Out of this experience, Jacob was empowered by a promise from God that he carried with him until his dying day:

And he dreamed, and behold a ladder set up on the earth, and the top of it reached to heaven: and behold the angels of God ascending and descending on it. And, behold, the Lord stood above it, and said, I am the Lord God of Abraham thy father, and the God of Isaac: the land whereon thou liest, to thee will I give it, and to thy seed; And thy seed shall be as the dust of the earth, and thou shalt spread abroad to the west, and to the east, and to the north, and to the south: and in thee and in thy seed shall all the families of the earth be blessed. And, behold, I am with thee, and will keep thee in all places whither thou goest, and will bring thee again into this land; for I will not leave thee, until I have done that which I have spoken to thee of (Gen. 28:12-15).

Everything in life is based on some sort of promise. It may be the mortgage for your house, a bank loan for your car, a job you have, or even the marriage relationship. All of these and many more aspects of life are contingent upon a promise. Every problem is the result of some broken promise, and every relationship depends upon promises made.

## Understanding God's Promises for Us

According to the Bible, God makes three types of promises to His people. First, there are limited promises. These do not apply to everyone, but rather to a particular group of people. God made certain promises to Israel that applied only to Israel. He made other promises to individual tribes within the nation of Israel.

Then there are the general promises of God, which apply to everyone. Among those promises are the commitments God has made regarding salvation. Salvation is available to all men, both Jew and Gentile. Anyone can access these promises.

Finally, there are specific promises made to individuals. Particularly in studying the Old Testament, we find that on occasion God would make a specific promise to an individual for a specific purpose. Consider, for instance, the account of Gideon and his fleece, found in Judges 6. God gave Gideon a specific promise that does not apply to anybody else.

We often sing a song that says, "Every promise in the book is mine, mine, mine. Every chapter, every verse, every line." This is a wonderful little chorus, but it is not really true. Not every promise in the Bible applies to me.

If you disagree, then perhaps you would like to encourage all the women in the church next Sunday morning to claim God's promise to Sarah that she would have a child when she was well past her childbearing years. That is rather ridiculous. Sarah's promise from God was a specific promise to a specific individual; it does not apply to anyone else.

I like to keep in mind that everything in the Bible is for me, but not everything in the Bible is about me. I need to have a degree of spiritual discernment to find out what God is really saying to me today. I accept the entire Bible—every chapter, every verse, every word—as the Word of God. Still, some things in the Bible do not apply to me personally. As the Holy Spirit guides me through this host of promises, I come to those that are meant for me. Apart from the faithfulness of the Holy Spirit, this could be a maze of confusion.

We must ask ourselves: *What is the purpose of God's promises? How do these promises affect my relationship with God and my walk with God each day?* Keep in mind: God's promises reveal everything we need to know about God—and more importantly, everything God wants us to be.

The first step in evaluating any promise is to find out who is behind that promise. A promise is only as good as the one making the promise. Is he able to deliver on his promise? What does this particular promise say about the one making it? Anybody can promise you anything, but the only legitimate promise comes from the person who is able to deliver. Not only is God able to deliver on His promises to us, but He also desires to do so.

Religion in general promises a lot, but time has proven that it cannot follow through on its boasts. Choose the religion you want and examine its promises; you will find out that it cannot deliver.

Christ fully delivers on each and every promise He makes. This is what makes the promises of God so exhilarating—as well as so necessary in my walk with Christ.

Just as the ladder Jacob saw in his vision went up from where he was into the heavens where God was, so too do God's promises bring us ever nearer to the presence of God. This was what Jacob discovered: "And Jacob awaked out of his sleep, and he said, Surely the LORD is in this place; and I knew it not" (Gen. 28:16).

## God's Promises Reveal Aspects of His Nature

In looking at the promises of God, from Genesis to Revelation, we see that there is a divine purpose behind each of them. God's promises are not God being capricious and promising arbitrary things to make His people feel good about themselves and happy. The promises of God are dynamic and deliberate—and when we accept them, our Christian life begins to ascend to levels of spiritual power we never knew before.

A closer look at God's promises reveals that they are of a twofold nature. First, every promise of God reveals aspects of God's nature and character that He longs for His people to know. Many people know about God. The problem is that few people know God as He desires to be known. It is one thing to know that God exists or to believe that there's "somebody up there who likes me"; it is quite a different thing to know this God on the deep level He desires.

God's promises open Him up to the worshiping heart. That is the focus of all His self-disclosures. God delights to be known— and the passion of every believer is to know Him more and more intimately each and every day.

Let me offer a few illustrations to show what I mean. Take, for example, the promise we have in 1 Peter 5:7: "Casting all your care upon him; for he careth for you." What does this promise tell us about God? Out of this promise, what is it that God wants to reveal about Himself?

This promise reveals to us a God who cares deeply about the things that burden us from day to day. God is interested in the intricacies of our daily life—not just the emergency times, when we are desperate or in danger. Of course, God cares about those times in our life. But this promise reveals to us a God who wants to be so intimate with us that He shares our day-by-day concerns and cares. He desires to identify so closely with us that we not only feel comfortable in His presence, but we also seek that presence with all our heart. This is certainly a promise for Christians to embrace enthusiastically!

Consider another example, found in 1 John 1:9: "If we confess our sins, he is faithful and just to forgive us our sins, and to cleanse us from all unrighteousness." Here again is a very simple promise from God. What does it reveal to us about God? What is God trying to say to us about Himself in this verse?

This is probably the most wonderful revelation of God that we could have: God is a forgiving God. He is both faithful and just to forgive us our sins. God does not forgive us because of any whimsical affection He might have for us—or any passing fancy that might change tomorrow. Rather, the forgiveness of God is based upon the unchanging character and nature of God—"I am the LORD, I change not" (Mal. 3:6)—and there is no sin God cannot forgive. God desires to reveal to us that His capacity to forgive is bigger than our capacity to sin—and that everyone has equal access to this forgiveness through the Lord Jesus Christ.

Let us look at one more illustration, from Proverbs 3:5-6: "Trust in the LORD with all thine heart; and lean not unto thine own understanding. In all thy ways acknowledge him, and he shall direct thy paths." Who has not taken refuge in this wonderful promise from God?

What God is trying to reveal to us about Himself in this promise is that He takes a personal interest in the pathway of our life. He desires to direct our path—and when He is directing our path, we can be assured of going down the right road in the right direction. God is personally interested in every step I take every day of my life, and He is trying to reveal to me through this promise that I can trust Him with the overall direction of my life. He will never let me down or lead me in the wrong direction.

The promises go on, each revealing something about God's nature and character that He wants us to know. To pursue these promises is to discover aspects of God's nature that resonate in our own nature.

As I bathe myself in God's promises, I begin to understand His heart and passion—not only for all mankind, but also directed especially towards me. Studying the promises of God found in His Word does not bring me mere academic knowledge; it is in the power of the Holy Spirit to reveal to me through these promises what God wants me to know about Himself. What a joy it is to begin to know God as He desires to be known! I do not want the world to define God for me. I do not even want religion to define God for me. I want the Holy Spirit to reveal God to me through the exceedingly great and precious promises He has given to me.

## God's Promises Reveal His Expectations

The second aspect of these promises from God is that they reveal His expectation of us. Each promise reveals something God is expecting us to be, do or become. We do not have to guess what God wants from us. We do not have to wait until we are on the other side to find out what God expected of us during our lifetimes. Through His promises, the Holy Spirit begins to reveal to us God's high expectation for our lives.

Let us look again at the same promises I used to uncover the character and nature of God. In these promises, we will begin to see what God is expecting of us.

Take the first example—1 Peter 5:7: "Casting all your care upon him; for he careth for you." What does this promise reveal to me about God's expectation of me?

From this promise, we see that God fully expects me to cast all of my care on Him. He expects me not to carry my own burdens, but rather to transfer that load completely onto Him. "Take my yoke upon you, and learn of me . . ." (Matt. 11:29).

How many of us try to live the Christian life by carrying our own burdens, as Pilgrim did in John Bunyan's classic work, *Pilgrim's Progress*? Like Pilgrim in the story, we are weighed down with every care the world has to offer. It seems that each care is like a magnet, attracting additional cares to attach themselves to us. From this promise, I see that God is fully expecting me to transfer all of those cares and the anxieties attached to them over onto Him.

How sad it must make God to see so many Christians not understanding His expectations. How grieved He must be to see us needlessly carrying burdens so heavy that we stumble and fall under their weight.

Now let us look again at the promise found in 1 John 1:9: "If we confess our sins, he is faithful and just to forgive us our sins, and to cleanse us from all unrighteousness." What is God's expectation of me here?

Quite simply, God expects us to confess our sins. He expects us to own up to our failures, faults, mistakes and short-comings—call them what you will—and acknowledge them to Him. We can hide things from friends and relatives, but nothing can be hidden from God. In fact, some translations of this verse suggest that it means we are simply to agree with God as to what is sin in our life. God expects us, according to this promise, to be open and honest with Him about the issues of our life. The better we come to know God, the more we are able to trust Him with all our confessions.

Those who have fulfilled this expectation of God have discovered that it empowers them in living for God. God fully expects us not only to confess our sins but also to walk in the glow of forgiveness. In the Old Testament, Joseph understood this when he told his brothers, "Ye thought evil against me; but God . . ." (Gen. 50:20). The "but God" element changes everything.

The third promise was Proverbs 3:5-6: "Trust in the LORD with all thine heart; and lean not unto thine own understanding. In all thy ways acknowledge him, and he shall direct thy paths." What is God's expectation of me here?

God expects me to trust Him—and not to trust myself in anything. We are not to try to second-guess God. We are not to try to lay out our own agenda. Rather, we are to trust God with all of the issues in our life. God expects that of me. He does not expect me to provide my own guidance and direction in life. He expects me to turn my future over to Him completely and trust the wisdom of the One who knows the end from the beginning.

Why is it that we find it so hard to fully trust God? Simply, we have not allowed the Holy Spirit to reveal to us God as He desires to be revealed. As we yield to the Holy Spirit, He will be faithful in exercising leadership in this area of God's promises. He will show us God as He desires to be shown and as we delight in knowing Him.

By bringing our lives into harmony with God's promises, we begin to understand our path into the heart of God. Just as Jacob's ladder ascended up toward God, so too God's promises lead us upward in our journey into the heart of God. These promises are the key in empowering us to be everything He desires us to be. When we understand who and what God is, as He desires to be revealed, we can then appreciate what He expects out of our lives each day.

Every problem in the Christian life is a result of misappropriation of God's promises. Many look at these promises and see only the shallow aspect of them—not the real depth that God desires them to see. The reason evangelical Christianity is in such a powerless position today is that they have not embraced the promises of God in the light of their importance from God's perspective.

Many are so caught up with the trends, technology, techniques and trivia of our time that they cannot appreciate the reality of God's presence in our life each day. The key to that reality is seen in the promises God has given us. Whatever fascinates us will guide us—so my prayer is that the only thing that will fascinate me is God and His marvelous glory.

# Thy Word Is Like a Garden, Lord
## Edwin Hodder (1837–1904)

Thy Word is like a garden, Lord,
with flowers bright and fair;
And every one who seeks
may pluck a lovely cluster there.
Thy Word is like a deep, deep mine;
and jewels rich and rare
Are hidden in its mighty depths
for every searcher there.

Thy Word is like a starry host:
a thousand rays of light
Are seen to guide the traveler
and make his pathway bright.
Thy Word is like an armory,
where soldiers may repair;
And find, for life's long battle day,
all needful weapons there.

O may I love Thy precious Word,
may I explore the mine,
May I its fragrant flowers glean,
may light upon me shine!
O may I find my armor there!
Thy Word my trusty sword,
I'll learn to fight with every foe
the battle of the Lord.

# 14

# THE POTENCY
# OF GOD'S WORD
# TOWARD
# HIS PEOPLE

*When I look into the heavens, O God, my heart leaps in praise and adoration of Thee—that Thou wouldst condescend to consider someone like me. In me is nothing desirable, and yet Thou lookest in my heart with great desire. Thy Spirit has revealed to me that which only He can reveal: Thy love and pleasure in me. In Jesus' name. Amen.*

God wrote the Bible as originally given, and it is a trustworthy Sourcebook of authentic truth. Everything that is here is true, but not everything that is true is here. You can learn everything from the Bible that the Bible teaches, but you cannot learn everything from the Bible—for the reason that the Bible does not teach everything, nor does it pretend to. The Bible teaches that which deals with redemption. It is a book interested in our rescue from sin and death, our moral rehabilitation, and our spiritual regeneration.

The deliberate purpose of the Scriptures is in keeping us right, making us useful, causing us to grow up into the maturity of a full-grown Christian, and having us prepared for the journey across into eternity. It is interested in all that; it is not, however, interested in geometry.

You cannot go to the Bible and learn geometry, but you can go to the Bible and learn that "God so loved the world that He gave His only begotten Son" (John 3:16). You cannot learn from the Bible how to bake a pie or send up a rocket, but you can learn from the Bible that "except a man be born again, he cannot see the kingdom of God" (John 3:3).

The Bible reveals the truth we need to know in order that we may be saved from sin, regenerated, morally and spiritually rehabilitated, and prepared for the day of the Lord. It is all here, and that is what I mean when I say the Bible is the only Sourcebook for our daily practice—the only final, authentic source of information concerning those things that have to do with our salvation.

## The Discoverable and Undiscoverable Truths of Scripture

Among the truths we find in the Scriptures are those that come to us as revelation. Revelation is the uncovering of truths that had not been before known—and that are undiscoverable.

Some things can be discovered. Scientists discovered the atom. A century before Christ's time, Lucretius wrote a book, *On the Nature of Things*, and told us that there were atoms. He thought atoms were tiny, hard bits of matter out of which everything was made—just as a concrete building is made out of tiny bits of sand and cement. You can break a thing down and find its tiny particles. He came wonderfully close to the truth about atoms, even though he did not have the benefit of modern scientific techniques and information.

Molecular structure and things of that nature are discoverable. Even some of the truths that we find in Scripture are dis-

coverable. While God inspired the Bible to be written and inspired those we read about in its pages to say things, often
those things could be discovered. For instance, David said:

> When I consider thy heavens, the work of thy fingers,
> the moon and the stars, which thou hast ordained;
> What is man, that thou art mindful of him? and the
> son of man, that thou visitest him? (Ps. 8:3-4).

This was an inspired utterance in that the Spirit of God
moved David to write this psalm, and it has a spiritual benefit
for us. But this is not revelation, because it is a reaction that
anybody could have—even an atheist or a communist. Any person could look up into the heavens and say, "When I look at all
of that space, what is man?"

As a counterpoint to the night scene he described in the
eighth psalm, in the nineteenth psalm David reflects on the
daytime sky: "The heavens declare the glory of God; and the firmament sheweth his handywork. Day unto day uttereth
speech, and night unto night sheweth knowledge" (Ps. 19:1-2).

In verse five he describes the sun, "which is as a bridegroom
coming out of his chamber, and rejoiceth as a strong man to
run a race." Seen from the earth below, that is exactly what the
sun looks like—the great, glorious bridegroom of the world
shining in his splendor.

Both psalms are inspired, but there is no particular revelation there. Anybody could say the same thing—that the heavens
declare God's glory and the firmament shows His handiwork.
That is a discoverable truth.

It may seem like a fine distinction, but there is a difference
between revealed truth—which is undiscoverable—and truth that
is discoverable, but nevertheless inspired, in that it is brought

into the Scriptures and becomes part of the inspired canon of divine truth. Nobody could have discovered, for instance, John 3:16: "For God so loved the world."

But to return to the psalms, look how much could be discovered here:

> The trees of the Lord are full of sap; the cedars of Lebanon, which he hath planted; Where the birds make their nests: as for the stork, the fir trees are her house. The high hills are a refuge for the wild goats; and the rocks for the conies. He appointed the moon for seasons: the sun knoweth his going down. Thou makest darkness, and it is night: wherein all the beasts of the forest do creep forth. The young lions roar after their prey, and seek their meat from God. The sun ariseth, they gather themselves together, and lay them down in their dens. Man goeth forth unto his work and to his labour until the evening (Ps. 104:17-23).

Any ordinary observer could see these things, and yet the Holy Spirit caused the man of God to write them down in this psalm. Weaving in truths that could be discovered with truths that were undiscoverable, he wrote this divinely inspired nature poem—perhaps the greatest nature poem in all the literature of mankind.

I hope I have not confused the issue too much. The Scriptures contain both observable truth and undiscoverable truth. The man of God says, as he gazes up at the stars and the moon at night, "What is man that thou art mindful of him?" It is a reaction anyone could experience—a truth that can be arrived at by way of observation and reasoning. But then you come to John 3:16: "For God so loved the world, that he gave his only begotten Son, that whosoever believeth in him should not perish, but have everlasting life." Here there is not only inspiration, but also revelation of truth that could never be discovered by the mind of man.

## The Glory and Rubbish of the Universe

As revealed in one of the psalms we have already considered here, David observed mankind through his human eyes, and then, by prophetic vision, saw the great Son of man. By a kind of double exposure, he gets them both in the picture: mankind as ordinary men and women, and then Jesus Christ as the great man who was born of woman that He might live among mankind. David says that God made mankind—and for that little while, the Son of man—a little lower than the angels (see Ps. 8:5).

Blaise Pascal, the great French mathematician and philosopher, wrote the following in his work *Pensées*:

Man is but a reed, the feeblest thing in nature. But he is a reed that thinks. It needs not that the universe arise to crush him. An exhalation, a drop of water, suffices to destroy him; but were the universe to crush man, man is yet nobler than the universe, for he knows that he dies, and the universe, even in prevailing against him, knows not its power.

He also said this:

What a chimera then is man! What a novelty! What a monster, what a chaos, what a subject of contradiction, what a prodigy! Judge of all things, feeble earthworm, depository of truth, a sink of uncertainty and error, the glory and the shame of the universe.

We do not have to like it, but it is there and we might as well face up to it. We are both the glory and the rubbish of the universe—but we never would have been the rubbish of the universe if we had not chosen the gutter. If sin had not entered the world and we had not fallen, we would never have been the rubbish of the universe. When our Lord is finished with His redemptive work, He will have made His people again the glory of the universe. He will come then to be admired in His saints and glorified in all them that seek Him.

Man is the weakest creature there is, but he is the only creature that knows how weak he is, and that's where his glory is. He is able to know how weak he is, and no other creature has such knowledge. If you were to ask a mosquito (which I consider to be a very weak creature—touch him and he's dead), "Are you weak?" I do not suppose he would say, "Yes." He does not know he is weak, and he could not answer you even if he did. He would not even know what you had asked of him. I suppose mosquitoes do not particularly like human beings. If mosquitoes talked, they would call us "the animal that swats" because that is the only thing they know about us. To mosquitoes, we are simply the creatures that swat them when they land on us.

Man is the unknown, the pitiful, the wonderful, the weak, the mysterious—and yet he is the only creature who knows that he is all this. Man is the only creature that sins, and yet he is the only creature that could know that he sins and laments his sin. Man is the only creature that laughs; he is the only creature that knows how foolish and inconsistent he is, and laughs at himself. He is the only creature that aspires because there's no other creature dissatisfied with himself. Man alone is dissatisfied with what he is and longs to become something more.

Man can go up and around the earth now and look down on it—because he is the only creature who aspires beyond his present reality. The other creatures are exactly as they ever were.

The only other creature that ever improves is the one that a man gets and crossbreeds. The Guernsey, Jersey, Holstein and Hereford cattle you see standing around in little clusters under the trees on hot days are crossbreeds. That is to say, careful breeding has made them what they are today. Man got hold of a poor, swayback heifer and bred her into something better. Then he took that offspring and bred it into something better, and so on until he arrived at these fine cattle. If a man can get hold of a thing, he will breed it up—because man alone aspires. Nothing else does. What does this indicate? It indicates that God made man in His own image. Man bears the image and likeness of God, and of nothing else can that be said.

Man is also the only creature that prays. God made man to worship; he is the only creature on earth made to commune with God in that way. The lion roars for his prey, and the bird builds its nest in the thickets. The stormy wind blows, and the snow falls, but snow does not pray, and neither does the bird, nor the lion, nor the stormy wind.

We, who do pray, can read into nature prayers, but they are not there until we fancy that they are. We hear the wind blowing, and we say that she is moaning her prayers to heaven—but this is nothing more than our imagination. The wind is just blowing; you and I are doing the moaning. Similarly, we say that the little bird dips his bill in the water and then looks up and thanks God for it, but the bird is merely putting his chin up so the water will run down. That is all. It's purely a mechanical thing. No bird prays.

Seen as a minute physical creature in the vastness of the universe, man is small indeed. Seen as a spiritual creature in the bosom of God, he is greater than all the winds that blow, all the mountains that rise, all the seas that flow, and all the rivers that run down to the sea. He is great because God made him in His own image. That's why the Son came among us as He did. Why would the eternal Son become a man? He was the Son of God. Why did He become the Son of man? Because the creature bearing the image of God had sinned; he had become the glory and the rubbish of the universe.

## Christ, the Head of Mankind

Christ came down in human flesh in order that He might get down as far as we were. If He had come into the world as a child of 10, there would have been 9 years unaccounted for. If He had come as a child of 5, there would have been 4 years unaccounted for. If He had started 1 year old, there would have been that first year unaccounted for.

Even if He had come as an infant by some miracle other than childbirth, there would have been 9 months unaccounted for. But, "therefore also that holy thing which shall be born of thee shall be called the Son of God" (Luke 1:35). Jesus went clear back to the original germ of human life, that He might know everything man knows and develop in the same way that any man grows—right up to full, blooming manhood.

He came down to where we are. If He had been born in a palace, there might have been those, born in huts and grass cottages, whom He would not have understood, but He was born in a stable in order that He might know the poorest that there are.

Christ is now the corporeal Head of the human race, and under Him, humanity is going to regain our lost sovereignty. "Thou hast put all things in subjection under his feet," wrote the writer to the Hebrews. "For in that he put all in subjection under him, he left nothing that is not put under him. But now we see not yet all things put under him" (Heb. 2:8).

Jesus came down that He might taste death for every man. That word "taste" does not mean to sample—as a child might taste food and then reject it. It means to experience. He experienced death for every man. He was born, grew to manhood, died, and rose again from the dead. He is saving His Church—that is, the redeemed, regenerated, blood-washed, forgiven people who compose the true Church. The true Church inside the false church. The Church that God acknowledges and approves within the vast Christendom that He rejects.

We do not yet see with our eyes all things put under Him; but by faith, we do see all things put under Him. Faith is a kind of sight, because faith sees what has not yet happened. If we have faith, we act as if we can see those things that we believe. If we claim to believe but do not have faith, we act as if we do not believe at all.

We say we believe in revelation. We believe in inspiration. We believe in man made in the image of God. We believe in God, who made in the image of man the incarnation of the holy Son. We say we believe that Christ tasted death for every man, in order that we might cease to be the disgrace of the universe and become the glory of the universe again.

Yet if we truly believe these things, we will begin to act as if we see them. Remember, you do not believe a thing rightly until you act in full accordance with it. When you bring your life into line with your faith, you are a believer, but when your life is not in line with your faith, you are no true believer at all. We believe that Christ tasted death for every man, and that He will soon triumph over all things and God will put all things under His feet. I believe that. I believe there will be a new heaven and a new earth, wherein dwells righteousness.

God is going to clean up His universe. When He comes, whose right it is to reign, and becomes Lord over all of His creation, there will be a new heaven and a new earth. The whole of creation, now under the bondage of depravity, awaits this great day. God is going to let the heat of His mighty presence burn up all the evil in order that He might replace it with all that is good.

"We see not," says the Holy Spirit, "all things under Him, but we see Jesus." God has put all things in subjection under His feet. We do not see it all done yet, but we have faith—and we see Jesus, who for a little while was made lower than angels in order that He might suffer death. We see Him crowned with glory and honor at the right hand of God the Father Almighty. When He comes back again, He will put all things under His feet.

For myself, with God's help, I want to live for that time. I want my money to live for that time. I want my talents, whatever they may be, to live for that time. I want my time to be given for that hour when He comes back again. I do not want to live for the earth while this time is approaching. I want to live for that day while it is approaching. I believe with all my heart that God has put all things under His feet, and that, one of these days, He is coming back to take His power and reign. *May God grant that you and I are ready. Amen.*

## Work, for the Night Is Coming
### Anna L. Coghill (1836–1907)

Work, for the night is coming,
Work through the morning hours.
Work while the dew is sparkling,
Work 'mid springing flowers.
Work when the day grows brighter,

Work in the glowing sun.
Work, for the night is coming,
When man's work is done.

Work, for the night is coming,
Work through the sunny noon.
Fill brightest hours with labor,
Rest comes sure and soon.
Give every flying minute
Something to keep in store.
Work, for the night is coming,
When man works no more.

Work, for the night is coming,
Under the sunset skies.
While the bright tints are glowing,
Work, for daylight flies.
Work till their last beam fadeth,
Fadeth to shine no more.
Work while the night is darkening,
When man's work is o'er.

# 15

# THE WORD OF LIFE

*Thy Word, O God, has brought to me everlasting life through Him who is the Word of Life. My sin has been my undoing and has made me out of sync with Thy glorious will. Thank Thee, O living Word, that upon my confession Thou art faithful and just to cleanse me of all my sin and bring me back into harmony with Thy blessed will. Amen.*

The apostle John, in his first epistle, uses the phrase "The Word of Life" to refer to Jesus Christ. That phrase has come to mean a great deal to believers down through the centuries. With it, John declares a truth about Jesus Christ that is absolutely essential to our daily Christian experience. This declaration concerns *Emmanuel*—God in the flesh.

John was quite familiar with the remarkable stories of what we now call Advent. He was there to witness it all firsthand: "That which was from the beginning, which we have heard, which we have seen with our eyes, which we have looked upon, and our hands have handled, of the Word of life" (1 John 1:1). John offers a personal testimony that cannot be lightly regarded.

We, too, are quite familiar with the Advent stories and focus on them once a year. Unfortunately, we have crowded around the first advent a lot of tradition and stories that seem only to take away from the real purpose of why Christ came. John takes the time to explain, from his perspective as an eyewitness, what the essential elements are and what we need to appreciate this far from the actual event. What he shares with us is not truth to be observed once a year and then put back in the attic with the rest of the seasonal paraphernalia. This truth energizes the Christian's daily walk.

John, the beloved disciple, begins his epistle with the phrase, "From the beginning." This is quite interesting, because it lays the groundwork for the understanding that the physical birth of Jesus Christ was not His beginning. The terminology here has to do with the eternity of Christ. John is giving witness to a manifestation, in a particular time, of that which is eternal. Paul says it a little differently: "But when the fulness of the time was come, God sent forth his Son, made of a woman, made under the law" (Gal. 4:4).

## Before or After?

The facts of Christ's eternity and incarnation give rise to any number of paradoxes. From a historical viewpoint, this Christ that John is writing about is the "Son of David"—and yet He antedates David. This is the marvelous inconsistency we find when we look into the person of Jesus Christ. How can a son born of a father go back prior to the birth of that father? Oh, the delightful incongruities we stumble over as God tries to deal with man's limited understanding! Only by faith can we wrap ourselves around this marvelous truth.

Then He is referred to as the "Seed of Abraham"—but he was before Abraham as well. Jesus said to the religious leaders, when they questioned Him, "Verily, verily, I say unto you, Before Abraham was, I am" (John 8:58). Imagine those old Pharisees, experts in the religious law, scratching their heads as they tried to figure out what Jesus had just said.

Christ is also referred to as the last Adam, but He dates back to before the first Adam. Trying to pin Christ down with a time sequence is impossible, because He existed prior to time. He rises above and beyond time. It was time that flowed from the mouth of this One who is referred to as the Ancient of Days.

Christ derives no glory from David or Abraham or Adam. All their glory comes from Him—and in giving them glory, He does not deplete any of His own glory. What He has, He has in unlimited supply. What He gives does not in any way lessen what He has. "I am Alpha and Omega, the beginning and the ending, saith the Lord, which is, and which was, and which is to come, the Almighty" (Rev. 1:8).

Christ is often likened to Aaron—but this parallel breaks down rather quickly. Aaron had a beginning, but Christ was "in the beginning." Aaron offered a sacrifice for his own sins, while Christ offered Himself for the sins of the world. Aaron took his glory from the priesthood, but Christ gave of His glory to others, such as Aaron. Aaron's priesthood came to an end, but Christ has a priesthood that is forever and ever—a priesthood that extends far into the unsearchable aspects of eternity, up in the rarefied atmosphere where time has no effect.

Whenever we tell a story, it always has three elements: the beginning, the middle and the end. When we come to the story of Christ, it is impossible to start from the beginning. John uses the word "beginning" in order to communicate to his readers some idea of what he is trying to say. Jesus Christ was from the beginning in the sense that He *was* before anything else began.

## The Living Word Made Manifest

John's declaration concerning Emmanuel starts with "from the beginning." Then, John moves on to declare this one who has come in the flesh to be "The Word of Life." The term John uses here applies to Jehovah. He is tying the Christ he witnessed and handled to the Jehovah of the Old Testament.

Moses, at the burning bush, queried God: "Behold, when I come unto the children of Israel, and shall say unto them, The God of your fathers hath sent me unto you; and they shall say to me, What is his name? what shall I say unto them?" (Exod. 3:13).

The response was, "I AM THAT I AM . . . Thus shalt thou say unto the children of Israel, I AM hath sent me unto you" (v. 14).

That was Jehovah—the timeless essence of all God is in His revelation to mankind. There is no better way to explain God. Many people spend a lot of time and use up a lot of words trying to explain who God is—and fail quite miserably. Language can only go so far; it cannot fully explain to us the mystery of that One we call Jehovah. This glory John is sharing with us— this blazing, effulgent idea from God. The eternal Logos of God, John declares, is among us.

His further declaration is that this Word of Life was manifest: "For the life was manifested, and we have seen it, and bear witness, and shew unto you that eternal life, which was with the Father, and was manifested unto us" (1 John 1:2).

John testifies that God came to where human beings could experience it. Christ manifested Himself in such a way that John and his fellow disciples could bear witness and testify that these things were true. Prior to this, man could only know about God. Now, as John declares, we can experience God on a personal level. We can know God as He delights to be known by His people.

That eternal Life became human flesh, and John boldly testifies that they heard, saw, looked upon and handled the Word of Life. I imagine that as John wrote this, his heart was filled with the awesome aura of that manifest presence. This is the goal of every Christian experience: to know God in His manifest presence—that same presence that stayed with John following his post-resurrection encounter with Christ in the upper room. From that moment on, there was something about Christ that filled his heart with joy unspeakable.

We, too, can experience the manifest presence of God as John describes it in his epistle. This is why the Scriptures are so absolutely essential and important in the Christian's life. As we come to the Word of God, we do not come just for information; we come for an encounter with the living Word of God. How some can just read a bit here and a bit there and then walk away is beyond my understanding. The cold textualism of many today borders on blasphemy. I will not settle for just the text. I want to see beyond that text and encounter the Christ—the Word of Life.

There have been times when I have lost myself in the manifest presence of the Lord as I meditated on His Word; He has come mysteriously close, defying explanation. If you can explain something to the satisfaction of logical reason, it is not God. We have not truly read the Scriptures until we have experienced the manifest presence of the Word of Life, even Jesus Christ.

What does all this reveal to us about God?

First, according to John's declaration, God is Life. Many seek to find the source of life, and most of those look in the wrong direction. But in the manifestation of the Word of Life, who is Jesus Christ, we discover the true source of life. We have been given eternal life through Jesus. Many speculate as to what is meant by the word "eternal" when it is associated with the word "life." Eternal life is a quality—not simply a duration—of life.

This life that God gives us is the essence of what He is. When God created us, He said, "Let us make man after our own image" (Gen. 1:26). This means that we have the capacity to receive from God that which is uniquely God: eternal life, which is a quality of life that rises above the elements of time and space.

This quality of life allows us to rise above the circumstances of our time and gaze into the smiling face of eternity. We are not living for this day or the next; we are living for all of eternity. We used to sing a Sunday School song that said, "With eternity's values in view, dear Lord, with eternity's values in view. May I live each day, dear Lord, with eternity's values in view." My life today, because I am a Christian, is reflective of the eternal quality of my Father which art in heaven.

John's declaration about this manifested Word of Life also leads us to the truth that God is Light.

I am talking about more than just a flashlight, a candle or even a spotlight. When we read that God is Light, we must understand that here is eternal Life contemplating itself. Here is absolute holiness in the purest sense of that word.

This Light is absolutely pure without any defilement at all. Perhaps there is a better word than "absolute," but I am not sure I can think of one. The purity of God is so absolute that its brilliance overcomes everything else.

No matter how dark and dismal the night has been, when the sun rises in the morning, it expels the darkness. The darkness cannot stand up against the light. Jesus Christ, the Word of Life, is the Light of the world, expelling the darkness of this present age.

Then John declares that God is Love. Here is eternal Life contemplating others. This Love goes forth in spontaneous kindness to rescue those who are perishing. It is the active movement of God toward sinners who do not deserve to be in His presence. Certainly, they cannot come to Him, but He of a surety can go forth to them.

As John declares Christ to be the Word of Life, he is telling us that God is Life and Light and Love. All of these aspects of Christ are manifested to us through the brilliance of God's Word, the Holy Scriptures.

## The Work of the Word of Life

What is the purpose of Christ's manifestation as the Word of Life? How does it affect us as believers and lovers of the Word of God?

The primary purpose is to bring God's life to man. Man was created in the image of God—and God, for whatever His reasons, pursues man with a tenacity unmatched anywhere in the created universe. God's great desire is to bring His life to every man, woman and child in this world. This is why He sent His Son into the world.

It is impossible to read the Scriptures for long without coming across the scarlet thread that begins in Genesis and continues all the way to Revelation. The great prayer in Revelation 4:11 says it all: "Thou art worthy, O Lord, to receive glory and honour and power: for thou hast created all things, and for thy pleasure they are and were created."

All of creation is "for thy pleasure." Here are three of the most wonderful words we can utter. To meditate on these words is to cultivate in our hearts love abounding. To kneel before God, knowing that my life brings pleasure to Him, is a very empowering thing.

John goes a step further than this. The purpose of the Word of Life is to bring us into God's fellowship. God does not stop at rescuing us; the purpose of that rescue is to enjoy fellowship with us. "Thou hast formed us for Thyself," St. Augustine said, "and our hearts are restless till they find rest in Thee." This explains the restlessness we see all across our world today. We were created for a purpose—and until we discover and fulfill that purpose, there is no rest for us. That purpose is to have fellowship with the God who created us for Himself. Those who choose instead to seek meaning in the elements of this world will never find any real satisfaction.

One more purpose of the Word of Life is to bring us into full conformity to God and His will. As I read and meditate on the Word, I begin to see areas of my life that are out of sync with the holy nature of God as revealed in the Scriptures. Then, by the help and grace of God Almighty, I begin to make changes.

If I look to the world, I will be fashioned in conformity to this world. If I look to the Word of Life, I will be fashioned in conformity to the will of God. That conformity will enhance my fellowship, not only with God, but also with fellow believers. If we are out of joint with anything in the Scriptures, it will show up in our fellowship with God and with one another. When we are close to the Shepherd, we will be close to a flock.

How do we deal with those things we find to be out of sync with the will of God?

The first thing is to acknowledge the sin that has been revealed to us by the Word. If we deny our sin, we are, as John explains in 1 John 1:8, deceiving ourselves. How many believers today are living a life of deception because they are denying some sin? If we deny our sin, we also show that the Word of Life is really not in us. The question is not how big or small the sin is. The question is simply whether some part of our life is out of sync with the will of God.

John goes on to say that if we confess our sins, God is faithful to forgive us and to cleanse us from all unrighteousness. He is eager to bring us into full conformity and fellowship with Him. God's Word draws me to Himself in order that my life will bring Him pleasure.

## Wonderful Words of Life
### Philip P. Bliss (1838–1876)

---

Sing them over again to me,
Wonderful words of life;
Let me more of their beauty see,
Wonderful words of life;
Words of life and beauty,
Teach me faith and duty.

Christ, the blessed one, gives to all,
Wonderful words of life;
Sinner, list to the loving call,
Wonderful words of life;
All so freely given,
Wooing us to heaven.

Sweetly echo the gospel call,
Wonderful words of life;
Offer pardon and peace to all,
Wonderful words of life;
Jesus, only Savior,
Sanctify forever.

Our dear Savior will come some day,
Wonderful words of life;
Come to rapture His Bride away,

Wonderful words of life;
Glory, glory, glory,
Shout the wondrous story!

Beautiful words, wonderful words,
Wonderful words of Life;
Beautiful words, wonderful words,
Wonderful words of Life.

# 16

# THE MYSTERY OF GOD'S STRANGE SILENCE

*I long for Thee, O God. The noise around me distracts me
from that still, silent voice within. Thou art speaking to me, and I
long to hear Thy voice. Help me to quiet myself to such a point
that I might hear Thee. May the noise of my generation and
the culture around me subside, so that I might hear Thee
speaking to me in that still, small, most mighty voice.
In Jesus' name. Amen.*

One of the most troubling questions for Christians down through
the ages has centered on the strange silence of God: *Why doesn't
God speak when we want Him to?* Not only is this something that
puzzles us today, but the question also plagued the great men
of God. Even David, a man after God's own heart, was per-
plexed about God's silence.

"Unto thee will I cry, O LORD my rock; be not silent to me:
lest, if thou be silent to me, I become like them that go down
into the pit" (Ps. 28:1).

But God has not always been silent, and He even speaks today for those who have ears to hear. Perhaps that is the problem. The vast majority of people today do not have ears to hear

the still, small voice of God. It was the great prophet of Jehovah, Elijah, who broke through the silence of God:

> And he said, Go forth, and stand upon the mount before the LORD. And, behold, the LORD passed by, and a great and strong wind rent the mountains, and brake in pieces the rocks before the LORD; but the LORD was not in the wind: and after the wind an earthquake; but the LORD was not in the earthquake: And after the earthquake a fire; but the LORD was not in the fire: and after the fire a still small voice (1 Kings 19:11-12).

As we read the Scriptures, we find God speaking, demonstrating and manifesting Himself to the people. Their secret was that they persevered until they heard that voice. In the Old Testament, God wrought mighty works in the sight of men. We read of how He miraculously brought Israel out of Egypt; we see how He provided for her through the wilderness area and protected her as He led her into the Promised Land.

## Hearing God in the Old Testament

All through the Old Testament are marvelous examples of God intervening in the lives of people—especially His people, Israel—making Himself real to their hearts and often interfering in nature and life. I could not possibly enumerate all of the illustrations of this, but let us consider just a few.

Elijah's contest, on Mount Carmel, with the Baal prophets is one instance of this manifestation of Jehovah. Elijah challenged these prophets to demonstrate the reality of their god, Baal. He wanted to prove to them that all of their boasting was nothing without a demonstration of power.

At one point Elijah mocked the prophets: "And it came to pass at noon, that Elijah mocked them, and said, Cry aloud: for he is a god; either he is talking, or he is pursuing, or he is in a journey, or peradventure he sleepeth, and must be awaked" (1 Kings 18:27).

Either Elijah was a fool or he was sure of his God. The rest of the story proves that the latter was true. Elijah knew God would demonstrate His power and authority to put down all of the worshipers of Baal. The horrific silence of Baal would soon be broken by the mighty voice of God. When God breaks His silence, all creation falls silent before Him.

In this and many other Old Testament accounts, one is impressed with the throbbing nearness of God. It is as Jacob realized when he awoke from his dream: "And Jacob awaked out of his sleep, and he said, Surely the LORD is in this place; and I knew it not" (Gen. 28:16).

Throughout the Old Testament, we see how God took an active part in His people's lives. From the deliverance of Israel from Egypt, to the wilderness miracles, and on into the conquest of Canaan—all of these are scenes where God personally interacted with His people. None of these experiences had any kind of logical explanation.

How do you explain the parting of the Red Sea?

Some have tried to put together some whimsical idea of how that might have happened, but really it was an act of God. It was God manifesting Himself to His people in a way that brought a sense of awe and reverence to them. The manifest presence of God hovering over the tabernacle throughout the years in the wilderness was also an indication of "God in the midst."

Then we read about the judges and kings of Israel. Time after time, we find God taking a man, like the young shepherd

David, and manifesting Himself through that man. Elijah and Elisha were examples of that. Explain their miracles, if you please. Tell me how these things happened. How did they do it?

Quite simply, it was God showing Himself to them—and through them—by taking an active part in their lives.

The Old Testament also teaches us that God's people were under His cloud of protection; nobody could touch them without first coming through Jehovah.

The story of Job illustrates this principle. Around Job was a "hedge" protecting him and his household. Even Satan recognized that phenomenon and could not penetrate it without God's permission.

> Then Satan answered the LORD, and said, Doth Job fear God for nought? Hast not thou made an hedge about him, and about his house, and about all that he hath on every side? thou hast blessed the work of his hands, and his substance is increased in the land (Job 1:9-10).

To those Old Testament saints, Jehovah was a reality in their lives, as His manifested presence was demonstrated to them in an impressive variety of ways. They took for granted that God would show up at the right time.

## Hearing God in the New Testament

The New Testament shows God working with increased zeal close to man and nature. This portion of the Scriptures begins with the conception and birth of Jesus Christ, the Savior. The Holy Spirit overshadowed the Virgin Mary, bringing into her body the seed of the living Word. The miraculous virgin birth begins a new stage of God's redemptive work among men.

If you review the life and work of Jesus, you will see a deluge of miracles at His hand. Each of these miracles was a specific demonstration of "God in our midst." Man cannot explain these works of God. We do not explain what we believe; we believe what cannot be explained in human terms.

Then we come reverently near to the cross where Jesus died. Heaven was very near earth that day. At one point, darkness enshrouded the area, so no man could see what God was really doing. It was a miracle—something beyond the realm of human possibility. Following Jesus' death came the resurrection, that miracle of all miracles.

In the book of Revelation, we have the declaration of this resurrected Christ: "I am he that liveth, and was dead; and, behold, I am alive for evermore" (Rev. 1:18).

Some have tried explaining the resurrection in human terms. Some have even tried explaining it away. But there it stands as a point in history defying human explanation—a monument of God's grace, power and redemptive purposes for mankind.

Following the resurrection of Jesus Christ, God revealed Himself through His Church to needy man. God had not given up on man and still intervened in the life of His people. In Acts 10:1-4, we read:

> There was a certain man in Caesarea called Cornelius, a centurion of the band called the Italian band, a devout man, and one that feared God with all his house, which gave much alms to the people, and prayed to God always. He saw in a vision evidently about the ninth hour of the day an angel of God coming in to him, and saying unto him, Cornelius. And when he looked on him, he was afraid, and said, What is it,

Lord? And he said unto him, Thy prayers and thine alms are come up for a memorial before God.

Cornelius saw in a vision an angel of God. Here was God revealing Himself to a man who was searching for truth. We see similar demonstrations all through the book of Acts.

In that Early Church, God was wondrously near to those who sought Him.

As we read further, we follow the exploits of the apostle Paul. Here was a man who lived in the presence of God on a daily basis. The more serious trouble he got into, the more Christ manifested Himself. At times, Jesus even came personally and stood with Paul during the night, giving him the assurance of the divine presence. The rest of the New Testament—the epistles and the book of Revelation—continually demonstrate God's intervention in the lives of His people. It seems the more difficulties a Christian or church got into, the more God demonstrated Himself to them. The motto of the Early Church was "God in our midst."

## Hearing God in Church History

Throughout Church history, we see countless examples of God working among those He loved: Augustine, Savonarola, Pastor Blumhardt, George Mueller, J. Hudson Taylor, D. L. Moody, A. B. Simpson—the list goes on and on. God showed Himself through these men in miraculous ways. Looking at their lives, we easily conclude that with them God was not silent at all. Through them, He spoke, moved and accomplished His purposes.

We then come to the great revivals—the Welsh revival, the move of God in Korea, the Great Awakening, and the revival in the New Hebrides, to name just a few. Read about these revivals and you will quickly see that God certainly was not silent during those times of refreshing. John and Charles Wesley shook the world with the revival God wrought through them. These revivals were times when God spoke clearly and loudly to His Church and through His Church.

In our own country, we witnessed a great move of God through Charles Finney. That austere Presbyterian was mightily used of God. Whenever Finney felt God's presence subside, he stopped everything that he was doing, went out into the woods, and fell on his face before God until the fire was rekindled in his own heart. God spoke loud and clear through Charles F. Finney.

A. B. Simpson lived a miracle almost every day of his life. God spoke through this Canadian-born evangelist loud and clear—and consequently the missionary work he began became one of the great missionary movements of modern history.

It saddens me to acknowledge that most people, even Christians, are total strangers to this kind of thing. They may read about the events I have just mentioned and yet not really understand that here were men and women through whom God spoke and was not silent.

## Four Realms of God's Work

A survey of God's interactions with His people reveals four realms in which He has historically worked.

First, God has moved in man's heart to save. This is the great blessing of God: to speak words of redemption and forgiveness to the human heart, and to see that person transformed by the power of the Word of God.

God has also worked wondrously to strengthen and to heal. The testimonies concerning this are too numerous and compelling to ignore. Now, I cannot deny that there have been false claims of healing and religious charlatans in this area, but these do not negate the fact that God speaks marvelous healing words to the bodies of His people.

God also speaks into man's struggle, offering words of encouragement and guidance. We live in a world diametrically opposed to the walk of the Christian. God speaks by the Word, and man's struggle takes on a new dimension. It is God's Word flowing through a life and touching the pathway of the Christian as he walks with the Lord.

God speaks the most dramatically when it comes to soul-winning labors. What Christ is interested in is seeing men and women come to know Him as their Lord and Savior. The words that God is speaking to the Church today are words of redemption; He is communicating to us His passion to bring men and women to a point of repenting of their sin and accepting Jesus Christ as their Lord and Savior.

Yes, God is speaking in our world today. Most do not hear, but those who do hear the still, small voice of God are enthralled by the dynamics of that voice in their life. God's voice touches every aspect of life and brings blessing, encouragement and strength in times of adversity.

Sadly, even many Christians are strangers to God in this area. His voice is conspicuously silent to them. Too many have been trained not to expect God to respond to them. Prayer has become just a ritual, void of any kind of expectation; it is something they go through because someone told them they need to go through it. They are strangers to the wondrous side of prayer: expectation. To pray without expectation is to misunderstand the whole concept of prayer and relationship with God. God is not silent. If I pray with the assumption that He *is* silent, my prayers have no value whatsoever.

The question I pose is this: *Are we enjoying the promises of God's Word in this area?* Specifically, let us consider these promises:

But seek ye first the kingdom of God, and his righteousness; and all these things shall be added unto you (Matt. 6:33).

If ye abide in me, and my words abide in you, ye shall ask what ye will, and it shall be done unto you (John 15:7).

Behold, I stand at the door, and knock: if any man hear my voice, and open the door, I will come in to him, and will sup with him, and he with me (Rev. 3:20).

But ye shall receive power, after that the Holy Ghost is come upon you: and ye shall be witnesses unto me both in Jerusalem, and in all Judaea, and in Samaria, and unto the uttermost part of the earth (Acts 1:8).

If any man see his brother sin a sin which is not unto death, he shall ask, and he shall give him life for them that sin not unto death. There is a sin unto death: I do not say that he shall pray for it (1 John 5:16).

God's voice is embodied in His promises. These promises are not like those a man might make, because each one has behind it the power of the One making the promise.

It is a startling thing to me that men can run a church without all of these promises and not seem to notice what they are missing. How can this be? We have before us the plain teaching of the Word of God. God is speaking. God is not silent. The mystery surrounding the silence of God is the mystery of unbelief.

I need to know what God is saying and that it is really He who says it. Then I must believe it, whether I understand it or not. I can never bring the counsel of the Lord to the judgment of my understanding.

The unbelieving world looks to see how we respond to God's voice. If we really believe what we say we believe, it will dramatically and dynamically affect our behavior. If our behavior does not match up to our belief, we are hypocrites and not true Christians at all.

## What Keeps Us from Hearing God?

Let us return now to our original question: *What causes God to be silent?* Scripture identifies four things that may prevent us from hearing the voice of God:

Thou hast not brought me the small cattle of thy burnt offerings; neither hast thou honoured me with thy sacrifices. I have not caused thee to serve with an offering, nor wearied thee with incense (Isa. 43:23).

But thou hast not called upon me, O Jacob; but thou hast been weary of me, O Israel (Isa. 43:22).

And he did not many mighty works there because of their unbelief (Matt. 13:58).

Behold, the LORD's hand is not shortened, that it cannot save; neither his ear heavy, that it cannot hear: But your iniquities have separated between you and your God, and your sins have hid his face from you, that he will not hear (Isa. 59:1-2).

Our sin, our unbelief, and our neglect of prayer and worship can all keep us from hearing God speak. But I come back to the question: *Is God silent?* The answer is unequivocal: no. The New Testament charter has never been abrogated; anyone who asserts that it has been must prove his claim, and this cannot be done. God still speaks through His Word to His people, just as He has always done.

> God, who at sundry times and in divers manners spake in time past unto the fathers by the prophets, Hath in these last days spoken unto us by his Son, whom he hath appointed heir of all things, by whom also he made the worlds (Heb. 1:1-2).

The question really is not: *Is God silent?* The question must be: *Am I hearing the voice of God?* If the answer comes back no, I must find a remedy. Scripture has told us what that remedy is. There is no mystery to God's silence; there is only a mystery as to why men would continue to live without hearing the voice of God.

## Be Still My Soul
Katharina A. D. von Schlegel (b. 1697)
Translated by Jane L. Borthwick (1813–1897)

Be still, my soul;
The Lord is on thy side.
Bear patiently the cross
Of grief or pain;
Leave to thy God
To order and provide.
In ev'ry change

He faithful will remain.
Be still, my soul;
Thy best, thy heavenly Friend
Through thorny ways
Leads to a joyful end.

Be still, my soul;
Thy God doth undertake
To guide the future
As He has the past.
Thy hope, thy confidence
Let nothing shake;
All now mysterious
Shall be bright at last.
Be still, my soul;
The waves and winds still know
His voice who ruled them
While He dwelt below.

Be still, my soul;
The hour is hast'ning on
When we shall be forever
With the Lord;
When disappointment, grief
And fear are gone,
Sorrow forgot,
Love's purest joys restored.
Be still, my soul;
When change and tears are past,
All safe and blessed
We shall meet at last.

# 17

# THE POWER OF THE HOLY SPIRIT ON THE WORD OF GOD

*In seeking thee, O God, I have encountered many counterfeits that have sought to hide Thee and Thy way from me. The way is foggy, with distractions and obstacles obscuring a clear vision of Thee. May I know the true work of God through the blessed Holy Spirit, and may my heart be open to the fullness of His work in me. In Jesus' name. Amen.*

Christian service and testimony are unique elements made effective by the power of the Holy Spirit working in our life through the Word of God. As one might imagine, since God uses these two elements for His purposes, the enemy of our soul strives to counterfeit them.

The only object worth counterfeiting is the original. Wherever I find a counterfeit, therefore, I look around for the original, which will not be far away. The enemy of Christ, in perpetrating this spiritual counterfeiting, seeks to confuse and divert people from the true path that leads to God.

So I would pose the question: *What is it that really makes my service for the Lord and my testimony of His grace powerful and effective?*

To understand this is to uncover the greatest secret of living the Christian life in contemporary culture. Our life must be influenced from the inside rather than the outside.

This is one criticism I have of contemporary Christians. They are more influenced by exterior things than by the interior work of the Holy Spirit. The Holy Spirit always works from the inside out, never the reverse. As I allow the Word of God to soak deep into my heart, the Holy Spirit will begin working on my inner being, giving rise to ministry and witness that flow outward, affecting the world around me.

How does this take place? Let's explore two elements of the work of the Holy Spirit in an individual's life.

## Moral Penetration

The first element of the Spirit's work is what I call moral penetration (see John 16:7-11). If my Christian service and witness are to be effective, they need to penetrate deep into the morals of a person.

The effect of this is to capture and arrest the soul's interest. This is the beginning of our service and witness. The people we are ministering to must be touched in this area of their life. Not many people are interested in spiritual things. After all, attention to spiritual things demands consecration as well as commitment. If my Christian witness is to be effective, it must reach deep down into the soul of the person to whom I am witnessing.

This work ultimately leads to a righteousness unattainable through the normal human channels—a righteousness that transcends mere human effort. This is a delicate process; the person must not be discouraged from seeking after righteousness, and yet must be brought to the understanding that the righteousness he seeks cannot be attained through human channels.

The Holy Spirit uses us to revive the conscience of the one to whom we are ministering. One ploy of the enemy is to so affect a man's conscience that it no longer functions. In reality, it is simply dead. It is the work of the Holy Spirit to touch that conscience and bring it to life again. Deep down inside of a man's soul lies that stupefied conscience—and the Holy Spirit wants to touch it and bring it alive.

The effects of this, of course, would be to terrify the heart. "Now when they heard this, they were pricked in their heart, and said unto Peter and to the rest of the apostles, Men and brethren, what shall we do?" (Acts 2:37).

This is the work of conviction in the heart of a man. Conviction is the harsh reality of my moral condition as seen from God's point of view. The enemy has been rather busy, at least during this generation, immunizing people from being horrified by their condition—or, as the Scripture says, "pricked in their heart." Hollywood has been busy making movies fortifying the human heart against such terror. Consequently, it is almost impossible to terrify the American public.

Conviction is necessary for true conversion; nobody can be saved without it. What God wants to do in the life of a person has to do with this work of conviction through the power of the Holy Spirit and the Word of God. The beginning work of the Holy Spirit is to pierce the moral area of the human heart.

The aim of this work is to point out what is sin. It is to identify and clarify sin from God's perspective. Out in the world, people have done away with sin—or at least have made it of such a nature that nobody fears sin anymore. It is simply doing as you please and having fun with it. After all, nobody is perfect.

Here is the point: There must be a moral penetration into the life of a person through the elements of Christian service and witness. Only the Holy Spirit, most often working through a Christian who is deeply committed to the Word of God, can do this.

## Spiritual Revelation

Following closely on the heels of moral penetration is the second element of the Holy Spirit's work: spiritual revelation.

> And the spirit of the LORD shall rest upon him, the spirit of wisdom and understanding, the spirit of counsel and might, the spirit of knowledge and of the fear of the LORD (Isa. 11:2).

> But when the Comforter is come, whom I will send unto you from the Father, even the Spirit of truth, which proceedeth from the Father, he shall testify of me (John 15:26).

> Howbeit when he, the Spirit of truth, is come, he will guide you into all truth: for he shall not speak of himself; but whatsoever he shall hear, that shall he speak: and he will shew you things to come. He shall glorify me: for he shall receive of mine, and shall shew it unto you. All things that the Father hath are mine: therefore said I, that he shall take of mine, and shall shew it unto you (John 16:13-15).

Here is the solemn logic of it all: No one can be saved until he believes in the eternal Son, and no one can believe in the eternal Son but by the Holy Spirit. The great mystery of the work of the Holy Spirit is that He chooses to do His work through committed Christians:

> Wherefore I give you to understand, that no man speaking by the Spirit of God calleth Jesus accursed: and that no man can say that Jesus is the Lord, but by the Holy Ghost (1 Cor. 12:3).

> He that believeth on the Son of God hath the witness in himself: he that believeth not God hath made him a liar; because he believeth not the record that God gave of his Son (1 John 5:10).

This is the clear teaching of the Scriptures, and there is no exception to it. Proof may be convincing to the intellect, but it can never enable the heart to believe. The target is a man's heart. That heart must be morally penetrated and experience a spiritual revelation. Apart from this, nobody can really come to know Christ.

## The Problem of Proselytism

Absent the working of the Spirit in men's hearts, we come upon the problem of religious proselytes. A proselyte is one who gives mental assent to Christ and becomes an adherent of the Christian faith.

Notice that I said "mental assent." This is the great danger of proselytizing. Men do it with the best of intentions, but it is a very dangerous thing to do. It has become the vehicle by which Satan hijacks people on the road to eternal life. Believe me, his driving license has not expired. It is part of the counterfeiting fraud the enemy has perfected.

How does religious proselytizing work?

People are persuaded to adopt certain beautiful and revolutionary views. The proselytizers can be very persuasive. This is how the cults work. They present certain views that are good and beneficial to mankind. Nothing is wrong with some of these views. The problem comes when they grip people and turn them into fanatical devotees. This is the core of every false religion and cult in the world today. I have no doubt concerning the sincerity and reality of the cults.

This devotion to attractive ideas is one reason for the rapid growth of cults around the world. Name any cult and you can find at its core this very thing. My concern is the inroads this has made in the evangelical church.

It is the great exchange—the trading of one value for another value:

No religion for religion.

Atheism for belief in the existence of God.

Buddhism for Christianity.

Catholicism for Protestantism.

The proselyte is talked into giving up one error in exchange for another.

We must realize the inadequacy and danger of proselytism. It has done untold damage to the kingdom of God by keeping people from a genuine conversion experience, which can only come from the Holy Spirit.

An imperfect conversion is more deadly than no religion. A short bridge that does not go all the way across the river is more dangerous than no bridge. The short bridge offers false hope, hiding the danger lurking just ahead. Proselytizing offers something, but not the full picture—the truth, but not the full truth.

Granted, an imperfect conversion may go far. Look at the success of the cults today. Many of them are doing good works and have fine reputations in this area. They certainly are the masters of the art of good works in our culture.

It may reform a person. Perhaps an alcoholic is enabled to attain a lifestyle of sobriety. Much can be done in reforming a person and helping him to overcome difficulties and problems in his life. This is commendable. But it does not go far enough.

An imperfect conversion may also refine a person's life. There is nothing wrong with taking off the rough edges of a person's life, refining him, and giving him a little bit of dignity. There is nothing wrong with helping a person to develop a positive attitude. Some people are negative all the time and need to have a positive change in their life. It is better, no doubt, to be positive than negative—but it is not good enough unless you are positive in the right things.

It also may give a person a new interest in life. A cult comes along and encounters an individual whose life is dreary and going nowhere. It contributes to significant changes in that life, bringing interest that awakens the person intellectually and emotionally.

It may even lead to sacrifice. Some of the cults are well known for sacrificial giving and living, much to the shame of the Christian Church today. Sacrifice is a simple price to pay for a fulfilling life. Sacrifice is giving up what I have for something I want. Everybody does it every day. (The problem, of course, lies in the defining of the phrase "I want.")

As good as all of this may seem on the surface, I must point out that the victims are more hopelessly lost than they were before. They are harboring a false hope that can only bring them to a disappointing end.

Woe unto you, scribes and Pharisees, hypocrites! for ye compass sea and land to make one proselyte, and

when he is made, ye make him twofold more the child
of hell than yourselves (Matt. 23:15).

Proselytizing goes far, but not far enough; in fact, it falls
dangerously short of what needs to be done in a person's life.
Religion can reform a person's life, but it can never transform
him. There is a lot to be said for reforming, but it does not
come close to the dynamics of transforming a person's life.
The Holy Spirit is the only guarantee of a transformed life.

My concern is that today's church work, missionary work,
evangelism, and publishing and writing of books and music are
no more than proselytizing. Many people have good intentions,
but their ministry does not rise above the level of mere proselytizing. Thinking that they are doing good, they are in reality
making a "shipwreck" of the faith of many people. Not going
far enough is the most devastating work of proselytizing.

How can we prevent this? How can we ensure that our
work, ministry and testimony rise above mere proselytizing?
The answer to that is simple: the Holy Spirit. The two acts of
the Holy Spirit I have described here—moral penetration and
spiritual revelation—guarantee that the work rises above what
the proselytizers are doing.

I cannot emphasize enough that these two works are the
master work of the Holy Spirit. Try as we might, we can never
duplicate what only He can do. Our lives should be so arranged
that the Holy Spirit is truly in charge, doing His work through
consecrated lives.

From my point of view, the evangelical church needs to
take notice here. The single greatest need of the church today is
simple: to be filled with the Holy Spirit—to work in Him and to
have Him work through us, using the Scriptures as His channel, to transform the lives around us.

## Arise, My Soul, Arise
### Charles Wesley (1707–1788)

Arise, my soul, arise.
Shake off thy guilty fears.
The bleeding Sacrifice
In my behalf appears.
Before the throne my Surety stands,
Before the throne my Surety stands;
My name is written on His hands.

He ever lives above,
For me to intercede,
His all redeeming love,
His precious blood to plead.
His blood atoned for all our race,
His blood atoned for all our race,
And sprinkles now the throne of grace.

Five bleeding wounds He bears,
Received on Calvary.
They pour effectual prayers,
They strongly plead for me.
"Forgive him, O forgive," they cry.
"Forgive him, O forgive," they cry,
"Nor let that ransomed sinner die."

The Father hears Him pray,
His dear anointed One;
He cannot turn away
The presence of His Son.
His Spirit answers to the Blood,

His Spirit answers to the Blood,
And tells me I am born of God.

My God is reconciled,
His pardoning voice I hear.
He owns me for His child;
I can no longer fear.
With confidence I now draw nigh,
With confidence I now draw nigh,
And, "Father, Abba, Father," cry.

# 18

# MOST SURE
# OF HIS PROMISE

*I love Thee, for I can trust Thee to always keep Thy Word.*
*All around me are those who fail to keep their promises for one reason*
*or another. Everyone at some time has disappointed me, but Thou,*
*O Christ, hast never disappointed me. Thou hast been as good as*
*Thy Word, and Thy Word hath been good to me. May I commit*
*myself this day and surrender my heart, mind and life to the promises*
*that have flowed into my heart. In Jesus' name. Amen.*

I have good news here for you from God. This news is like healing to the soul. It is better than any news from a far country—
better than any news you could hear or read about happening
in the world today. It is here by the Holy Spirit and it is for us.

The purpose of the Spirit is to confirm the Christian in the
faith. The Holy Spirit is saying to us: *This faith of Christ is worthy
of your complete confidence. It is worthy of your loyalty and your ultimate commitment.* He is saying to us that this faith of Jesus
Christ rests upon the character of God. I should like to emphasize that our Christian hope rests upon the character of the tri-
une God. We are saved through a new covenant.

If Christians could only keep in mind that we are covenant
persons! We are covenanters—as were those in Scotland who
years ago took that name—saved through the new covenant.
God has made a pledge of His own free will. A Christian is a

Christian—and remains a Christian—because a bond exists between the Persons of the Godhead and the believing man. God gives an assurance of His never-ending goodwill.

The eighty-ninth psalm describes the covenant that God makes with people. It refers to David, but it goes beyond David. He is talking about David's greater Son, and Heir, Jesus Christ the Lord.

In this psalm, we find statements made by God about David and David's seed and David's people—and they are almost unconditional. God never makes any unconditional promises, but these are as near unconditional as they ever get.

> My mercy will I keep for him for evermore, and my covenant shall stand fast with him. . . . My covenant will I not break, nor alter the thing that is gone out of my lips (Ps. 89:28,34).

Let me remind you that these promises are of value only as we can establish the fact that the One who made them is worthy. A promise is nothing in itself; its value depends upon the character of the one who made it.

If you make a promise you cannot keep—or do not intend to keep—it is of no avail and of no value. If you make a promise with the intention of keeping it, and you can keep it, then it is a good promise, because it rests upon a good character. Therefore, all the promises of God rest upon the character of God.

That is why I keep teaching and insisting that we ought to know what kind of god our God is. We need to know the God behind the promise. We ought to search the Scriptures and learn who this God we are dealing with is, so that our faith will spring up normally and naturally. If we know God, we will know when we are listening to a promise uttered by Him that

that promise is absolutely trustworthy—because the God who made it is trustworthy.

## Man's Promises Fail

There are different reasons that promises may be broken or fail. Let me give you some of those reasons.

Sometimes the person making a covenant does not intend to keep it. In such cases, the promise fails because of the duplicity of the promiser. He does not intend to keep his promise; he simply makes it in order to gain something. As soon as he has gained that thing, he breaks his promise. When it comes to God, I hardly need say that nothing like this could happen.

Another reason covenants sometimes fail is that the one who made the covenant finds it impossible to fulfill. A man makes a promise, but then things go badly for him socially, intellectually or financially, making him unable to fulfill his promise. This man fails through ignorance. He did not know his situation. He overestimated his ability, and that is why the promise is not kept. His intention was fine—he wanted to do the thing he promised—but he could not follow through.

A covenant may also fail because the one who makes it changes his mind and cancels it afterward. So the promise fails through the instability of the promiser. Maybe he had second thoughts or buyer's remorse.

Sometimes circumstances will shift a little bit, and people will become unable to fulfill the promise made, in which case it fails through the weakness of the promiser—as a result of circumstances the promiser is unable to control. Or a person makes a promise and then dies, so it fails through the mortality of the promiser. Before the promise can be made good, death comes knocking.

These represent the basic reasons covenants are made and broken—why covenants between men and men, or nations and nations, are sometimes wrenched violently apart. Unlike the promises of men, God's covenant cannot fail, and we are given the reason given for that.

## God's Promises Cannot Fail

Among men, an oath is an appeal to something greater. For instance, when a man wants to stand before a court and declare that he will tell the truth, the whole truth and nothing but the truth, he adds, "so help me God." That is considered an oath. After that, he is a perjurer if he tells a lie, because he has called upon somebody greater than himself to witness that he is telling the truth.

Men know their failures—in particular, in this case, their tendency to lie. Until you become a Christian and put away evil, lying is quite a convenient scheme for getting along in the world.

Men know this, and so they are not willing to have one of their own stand up and say, "It's this way."

Instead, they bind him by an oath, saying, "First put your hand up, and place your other hand on a Bible, and promise before this judge and all this court that you will tell the truth, and then call on God to witness that you're not going to lie."

This is rather humorous; I think they must chuckle in hell whenever a man gets up before a court and says, "I promise before God that I won't tell a lie." *Why were you not willing to tell the truth in the first place?* That is the question I would like to ask. I am always bothered when a man has to appeal to somebody higher than himself for confirmation that he speaks the truth.

God wanted to humble Himself and go along with our way of doing things, so He made a promise to Abram (see Gen. 15).

But who could He call on to confirm His statement? He could not appeal to an archangel. He had to appeal to something greater—somebody greater—and He looked about for greater and, of course, found none. So God swore an oath (see Heb. 6:17-22), but He could only swear by Himself.

He did this for the heirs of the promise. We say to God, "O God, what assurance do you give that Christ's death for us avails? What assurance do you give that the blood of Jesus secures our salvation? What assurance do you give that our place in Thy love is unchanging? What assurance, O God, do you give that our faith in Thy promises is secure?"

God replies, "I have nobody greater that I can call on. I cannot raise My hand and call on some god greater than Myself, because none greater exists, so I swear by Myself that I will do these things." That is an oath of confirmation.

As with any promise, the value of an oath depends entirely on the character of the one who swore that oath. Many a man swears an oath, and then sits there and lies, because he does not have any character to start with. He will not only lie out of season, but also swear and lie in season, because he has no character.

Because God is who He is, we can trust Him absolutely. Our hope of salvation, forgiveness, peace in death, and joy in the life to come does not rest on how we feel right now. If any of these things rested on how we felt this morning, we might as well pack up and head for the nether regions, because we do not feel heavenly—our mood is batted about by changing weather, hard work, and so on.

Our covenant—our hope—does not depend on how we feel. It depends on something else, something much greater. It depends upon whether or not God is right. It depends upon whether God is trustworthy to keep the promises He makes. It depends upon whether He is able to make good on His promises and keep His covenant. This is the definitive question.

## What We Know About God

Let us consider what we know about God. Holiness is one of the attributes of God. Because God is holy, He cannot lie. We can trust the immutability of God's covenant because it is impossible for God to lie. Some things God cannot do, even though He is omnipotent. God cannot lie, because God is holy. To lie, He would have to violate His holiness. God cannot violate His holiness; therefore, God cannot lie.

"Since God cannot lie," someone asks, "does that mean that He is not omnipotent?" The answer is that omnipotence is not the ability to do anything; it is the ability to do anything He wills to do. He does not will to lie. He does not will to cheat, nor to deceive. He does not will to play false with His people. God wills to be true to His children, and because He is holy, they are safe.

God is perfect in wisdom. Because our own understanding is so limited, we imagine that God could conceive a scheme to redeem men, and we might get some of those men to agree with Him and come His way and fall in with Him and believe on His Son—and then suddenly it would be found that God could not make good because He had misjudged something. But that is not possible.

God knows everything that can be known. When He makes a promise, He is able to make good on that promise because of who He is. He is perfect in wisdom and knows all the details—the end from the beginning.

If God were not omnipotent, He could not guarantee His ability to keep His covenant with me. If God were not omnipotent, I could not be sure I would be saved. I would think that I was saved, but when God reached a point where somebody was stronger than He, I would be lost. Knowing that "the Lord God omnipotent reigneth" (Rev. 19:6), and knowing that omnipotence means God can do everything He wills to do, I have no doubt at all about my salvation, for I am in the arms of the omnipotent God who has sworn to save me.

Suppose God were in the habit of changing His mind. I have met men who were always starting something new and then changing their minds about it. I would see them one day, and they would be all red-faced and flushed and excited. They could hardly eat for talking—telling me about their new project. I would shake their hand and wish them well. When I saw them two years later and inquired about that great work they had started, they would say, "Oh, that? It didn't go through."

God is immutable. When He promises something, that promise will be kept. He has assured us that we will be blessed forever; that His mercies will be upon us forever; and that we will not perish, but will be kept by Him. God, the immutable, does not change His mind about these things—or anything.

## Saved by a Covenant

Human covenants sometimes fail through the mortality of the promiser. A man makes a promise with every intention of keeping it, then grabs at his chest and tumbles over. They take him off to the hospital, and in a few days, he is gone. He meant all right. He was wise enough to do the thing he promised, and kind enough to want to do it, but he did not live to do it. The covenant that keeps you and me, unlike promises made by mortal men, is made and kept in being by the eternal God.

God cannot fail by cessation or discontinuance. God, the eternal God, lives on—and because He lives on, we live on. We live on as long as He lives on. Isn't this an awful thought, my brethren? Isn't it an awful, a wonderful, and an awesome thought?

We are going to live as long as God lives. We did not begin when God began, because God never began, but we did. However, going forward, as long as God, the eternal God, exists and continues to be—as long as God can say, "I am and continue to be what I am"—you and I will in the grace of God continue to be what we are, because we are saved by a covenant, sworn to by an oath.

> Wherein God, willing more abundantly to shew unto the heirs of promise the immutability of his counsel, confirmed it by an oath: That by two immutable things, in which it was impossible for God to lie, we might have a strong consolation, who have fled for refuge to lay hold upon the hope set before us (Heb. 6:18).

Those familiar with the Old Testament know what the phrase "fled for refuge" means. Israel had six cities set apart as cities of refuge. When a man accidentally killed another man, a law in Israel said that the "avenger of blood"—the next brother, the father or the next relative of the dead man—could take vengeance on this fellow.

The fellow that had the ax head would take off as fast as his legs would carry him, racing to the nearest city of refuge. Sometimes he barely made it in, with his tongue hanging out, panting like a tired dog, and the would-be avenger just behind him, almost within reach of the back of his neck.

He raced in, the court trial took place, and it was decided whether or not the man was to blame. If he was not to blame, then, of course, the dead man's relative could not take vengeance—to do so would violate the law again, and now he would be the murderer. That was the city of refuge. The man of God who wrote the book of Hebrews, being a Jew, knew all about these cities.

Whether a man was guilty or not, he had a right to fly to that city of refuge. If he was not guilty, that would be proved. But even if he was guilty, he still had a right to go to that city of refuge. If he made it to that city before his pursuer got to him, then he was safe.

The man of God says that we "have fled for refuge," and I can just see myself, with the devil one hot jump behind me, racing for the cross of Jesus, racing for Calvary's holy mountain. Just as I come panting in, the doors let down behind me, and the devil runs head-on into the gate and bounces off. He does not get me, because I have found the refuge and I am safe.

## The Anchor of Our Soul

The writer of Hebrews continues with another assurance: "Which hope," he says, "we have as an anchor of the soul" (Heb. 6:19). It is a sudden change of figures of speech. One moment, we are running to the city of refuge to lay hold of this hope, and in the next breath it becomes an anchor of our souls. But no matter. Let us explore now this new way of picturing the security we have in the promises God has made to us.

Picture a ship, with a storm coming upon it and the saints of God on board the ship. Somebody says, "What I see coming up out there, that typhoon, I think we're all dead. We're all sunk because we'll be blown on the rocks."

Somebody else says, "Look down there!" and you look down and try to see the anchor—and even though it is too far down for you to see it, your anchor grips to the rocks, and the ship outrides the storm. The anchor is there, though you do not see it. So said the Holy Ghost through the man of God whose words He inspired. We have an anchor that keeps the soul steadfast and sure while the billows roll. That anchor we do not see, but He is there.

The writer of Hebrews concludes the sixth chapter of his epistle with this: "Which entereth into that within the veil; Whither the forerunner is for us entered, even Jesus, made an high priest for ever after the order of Melchisedec" (vv. 19-20).

What does he mean by the forerunner entering in for us? It means that where Jesus is now, we are going to be. He is the forerunner. He went first . . . for us. We are coming along after Him, and where He is, we are going to be.

Then there is this final bit of good news: Jesus—our forerunner, anchor and refuge—is made a High Priest forever. In olden times, high priests kept dying, but this High Priest has life forevermore after the order of Melchisedec.

*So,* says the Spirit, *go on; keep on believing. You are not mistaken in fleeing to Christ.* Our hope is sure, our consolation is strong, and our forerunner has already entered. The anchor grips the rock. Everything is all right in our Father's house. So, arouse you. Pursue holiness. "Be not slothful, but followers of them who through faith and patience inherit the promises" (Heb. 6:12). Show diligence and full assurance of hope unto the end.

The Holy Spirit never exhorts until He has informed. He never gives an invitation until He has presented the truth. He lays before us one glorious, everlasting covenant sealed by blood, sworn to by God, and promised by the God who cannot lie. Then He says, *Because this is true, therefore show diligence. Because everything is all right on God's side, everything will be all right on your side—if you will only trust, have faith, believe, and put yourself in His hands—for He is where you are going. Because He is where He is, you are going where you are going.*

You are saved by an oath of almighty God. Because He could not appeal to a higher court, God appealed to Himself and said, "Surely blessing I will bless thee" (Heb. 6:14). Saving, I will save. Keeping, I will keep.

Christians ought to be the most delighted, happy people in the world. It is strange that we are not—but I know why we are not. The devil is out after us. The flesh is out after us. The world is out after us.

In fighting these three enemies, sometimes we do not have time to be happy. We do not have time to remember that we are as safe in the arms of Jesus as if we had been in heaven a thousand years—if we will only believe, go on, and not disgrace ourselves in the kingdom of God by turning back to the beggarly elements of the world. I do not think you will, for I am persuaded to believe better things of you, my brethren—things that accompany salvation.

We have a promise we can count on, because we have a Promiser who has never and can never fail.

## We Have an Anchor
### Priscilla J. Owens (1829–1907)

Will your anchor hold in the storms of life,
When the clouds unfold their wings of strife?
When the strong tides lift and the cables strain,
Will your anchor drift, or firm remain?

It is safely moored, 'twill the storm withstand,
For 'tis well secured by the Savior's hand;
And the cables, passed from His heart to mine,
Can defy that blast, through strength divine.

It will surely hold in the Straits of Fear—
When the breakers have told that the reef is near;
Though the tempest rave and the wild winds blow,
Not an angry wave shall our bark o'erflow.

It will firmly hold in the Floods of Death—
When the waters cold chill our latest breath,
On the rising tide it can never fail,
While our hopes abide within the Veil.

When our eyes behold through the gath'ring night
The city of gold, our harbor bright,
We shall anchor fast by the heav'nly shore,
With the storms all past forevermore.

We have an anchor that keeps the soul
Steadfast and sure while the billows roll,
Fastened to the Rock which cannot move,
Grounded firm and deep in the Savior's love.

# 19

# AN OPEN
# INVITATION

*O God, I have been the worst of men; therefore let Grace
triumph to the chief of sinners and make me to be the most
useful of men. In Jesus' name. Amen.*

I have tried in this book to outline as simply as possible the dynamics of God's power. Many have misunderstood what this divine power is all about, including some in biblical times. Peter wrote, concerning certain responses to the writings of the apostle Paul, "As also in all his epistles, speaking in them of these things; in which are some things hard to be understood, which they that are unlearned and unstable wrest, as they do also the other scriptures, unto their own destruction" (2 Pet. 3:16).

The foundation of God's power is the Bible, the Word of God. I want to make it perfectly clear that the Bible's purpose is not to replace God, but rather to bring us into the manifest presence of God. If we have read the Bible and not encountered the living Word, we have not read the Bible.

The Bible cannot be treated like some book of literature. The Bible is the bestselling book of all time, and yet it is the most misunderstood and undervalued book in all the world. The mission of the Word of God is to find us, identify us and the times in which we live, and show us what is wrong with us as well as what is right with us.

The Scripture's mission is to find us—and when the Bible says we are lost, it is exquisitely accurate in what it says. We are lost. The world is lost, and we do not know where we are.

## An Open Invitation

I want to close this topic by giving an open invitation. This invitation has to do with the Bible and our relationship to it.

In our Sunday School class, the children sing a little chorus that is much more than just a little chorus: "The B-I-B-L-E, yes, that's the book for me. I stand alone on the Word of God, the B-I-B-L-E." This, I say, is more than just a little Sunday School jingle. It encapsulates a truth that is vitally important for vibrant Christian living. The one line, "I stand alone on the Word of God," is the most important truth that we can know.

The Bible is our standard. Everything we do, think or say has to be in absolute harmony with the Word of God. Mark Twain said, "A classic is a book on everybody's library shelf, but a book nobody reads." I wonder if this cannot be said of the Bible today. But the Bible is not a relic to be revered; it is a book to be lived—and it can only be lived by the power of the Holy Spirit.

Leaf through the average Christian's Bible and take note of all the underlined passages. From these passages, you might think that God is a soft, spineless, moral Santa Claus, full of pity with no justice or judgment at all. That is because we typically choose to focus on passages that please us rather than those that threaten us.

A heretic is someone who selects the passages that he wants to believe. If you go through your Bible, selecting passages that please you and disregarding those that don't, you could be in the class of a heretic. It's not that you believe false doctrine, but you are not giving attention to the whole Word of God. It is a bit like living all the time on cake. Cake it not necessarily bad, but you have to have some other things to balance out your diet. The same thing goes with the Bible.

Certainly, we should not always be negative. Some people have nothing to say unless it is negative. Such is not the tenor of the Bible. The Bible faithfully points out not only what is wrong, but also what is right about us.

I am afraid that in our eagerness to make things better, Christians sometimes overlook what is right. This is never good. We should always acknowledge what is right with us. God is faithful in pointing out what is right with us and where we should abide in confidence as we walk with Him.

Allow me to point out that I do not think there is anything right about popular religion, as we know it today. There is nothing right about the sinner. There is nothing right about someone who acts as if significant passages of Scripture did not exist.

The Bible is faithful in bringing our time into focus so that God can pronounce a judgment or an approval. A unique felicity and wonderful ability of the Word of God is to reveal the nature and character of our times.

Many buy into the false notion that times change. We have new cars, new clothes, new homes and new technology. With all that is changing around us, somehow we have the idea that we are living in "new times." The Bible acknowledges no such thing. Man, as the fallen man he is, is the same, generation after generation. Sin does not change. I have mentioned this before, but let me reiterate it: Whatever is new is not true, and whatever is true is not new.

The Bible speaks to our times, because our times are greatly affected by the nature of sin. It is the business of the Word of God not only to tell me when I am right, but also to point out what I am doing wrong. Growth cannot take place unless there is judgment on those things in my life that are wrong.

## Allowing the Word to Work in Our Lives

While I do not recommend a continual evaluation of ourselves, I do suggest that we commit ourselves to the Word of God. Since the mission of the Holy Scriptures is to examine us and take our pulse—to settle on our spiritual health and pronounce or prove or condemn or command or warn or encourage—I recommend we spend considerable time with the Word of God.

My recommendation is that we take a little time out with morning devotions—more time than usual, perhaps. Take a longer time to read and really search the Scriptures. Let's get on our knees and put everything aside—all of these marginal notes and everything else—and let the Holy Spirit begin to talk to us.

I believe it might be possible even to have too many Bible translations around. Do not let the vast number of versions overwhelm or discourage you. Get a plain text Bible and just read the Word of God. Allow the Holy Spirit through that Word to speak into your heart.

As you read, I invite you also to do certain things that would advance your relationship with God. The primary thing would be to assess yourself: *Is there any rebellion in my heart?* Rebellion, according to the Old Testament, is as serious as the sin of witchcraft. Never take this lightly. Seriously evaluate your heart; is there the slightest bit of rebellion in your heart? If you find any rebellion, deal with it as firmly as you possibly can.

We must walk in the will of God. The will of God is the health of the universe, the harmony of heaven, the peace of paradise, and salvation itself. The will of God is light. The will of God is everything a moral being can want—and bucking God's will in anything, even the littlest thing, will bring dire consequences. Always remember that the will of God is your safety.

To know God's will and to walk in that will is the epitome of strength and safety in this world of rebellion against God Almighty. All your prayers, all your faithful attendance at church, and all your good works will mean nothing apart from this. It is simply whistling by the cemetery; it is talking big to hide our shameful fears.

In the Old Testament, Israel was a rebellious people who misplaced their confidence and put it elsewhere than in God and His will. We know the story of Israel. It seems to me that the evangelical church of today is replicating the errors made by Israel, as well as the errors found in the Pharisees and Sadducees in the New Testament. These religious leaders took confidence in the fact that they knew the truth, but the sad side of the story was, they did not walk in the truth. If what you know does not change how you walk, what you know is not very important.

I have often wondered why some Christians are always at church, at prayer meeting, requesting prayer, reading and carrying their Bibles, eager for orthodoxy, ready to defend the truth—and yet are the grouchiest and meanest and nastiest and hardest-to-live-with people in the whole world. They know the truth, and could quote it verbatim, but it did not change how they live.

Some people are spiritually cross-eyed. They are focused in two directions at the same time: looking one way but going another way. Too many Christians are just spiritually cross-eyed—untruthful and unbelieving, yet some of the most pious people in God's green earth. They insist on hearing religious talk all the time, and yet there is no humility among them.

Humility is a beautiful thing wherever it is found, and pride is heinous wherever it is found. These religious people always want to hear religious talk, and yet they never hear the real voice of God. I believe this is ironic.

## Evaluating Our Times

How shall we evaluate our times? I wish I could say we are in a time of great revival. I wish I could testify and say I thought things were looking up. But when I compare the times with the plain and clear teaching of the Bible, I cannot say that.

Present-day Christianity has all but done away with the warnings found in the Scriptures. Book after book has been published on the positive, wonderful side of Christianity, to the neglect of what is wrong with us. If I went to a doctor, and he simply patted me on the head and told me I was a wonderful person and that I should take things a little more cheerfully, I am not sure I would want to go back to that doctor. If all he could see was what was right about me, and never what was wrong with me, what kind of a doctor would he be?

I believe we need to know what is right about us. But I also believe we need to know what the Bible says is wrong about us, and then do something about it. If we are going to assess ourselves truthfully, we need to know both sides of the issue. Present-day Christianity is only taking one side of the issue. We need to deal with what is wrong—and you cannot deal with what is wrong unless you know what is wrong. The only way we are going to discern that which is wrong among us is by appealing to the Word of God: "I stand all alone on the Word of God."

I pray earnestly for the evangelical church today, that there may come a willingness on our part to hear the whole counsel of God. Once we have committed ourselves to listening to God's Word, we will begin to see the areas of our life that need judgment. The Scriptures emphatically say that judgment begins with the house of God: "For the time is come that judgment must begin at the house of God: and if it first begin at us, what shall the end be of them that obey not the gospel of God?" (1 Pet. 4:17).

The evangelical church in America, over the last generation, has committed enough sins to bring the whole building down on us. I do not exclude myself from this assessment. As evangelical Christians, we need to deal with the sins among us—personal sins and corporate sins both. We need to come back to the biblical definition of sin. According to the Bible, sin is any rebellion against God.

I am afraid that we have it too good these days. It does not cost much to be a Christian. We have become lazy and soft, and we have produced a generation that is self-assured, rebellious and caustic.

In the last few years, Christianity has become a show whose focus is entertainment. We are trying to beat the world at its own game; we are losing and not realizing that we are losing.

My heart's cry is that I want God back again. I want God back in our worship services. I am tired of worship services that are simply jazzed-up religious entertainment. I want God back in the middle of all that we are doing today. In order for that to happen, we need to assess ourselves and deal with those aspects of our life that are out of harmony with the Word of God.

Doctrine is not enough. No other generation has had the clarity of doctrine and theology this generation has. There are more Bible colleges and seminaries in the world today than there have ever been throughout the history of the Church. We know doctrine. We can quote doctrine. The problem is that our doctrine is just an academic thing. Our doctrine is just an appendage on our Christianity. People are finding out that doctrine is not really leading them to God—and if it does not lead us to God, of what value is it? If the doctrine we hold does not bring us into the presence of God, how does it really benefit us?

I want to be a part of the Fellowship of the Burning Heart. I want to so evaluate my life that I may weed out of it everything hindering me from coming into the manifest presence of God Almighty. I want God in my life. I want my life so arranged that God is at the center of it.

I invite you to evaluate your own spiritual life. Does it hold up to the scrutiny of the Bible?

## The Choice We Each Must Make

Which side are we on? Are we on the side of those who simply want to take it easy, or are we on the side of those who have been found and prophetically situated so we know where we are? Are we willing to separate ourselves from the poor, dead churches with their poor, dead entertainmentism?

The power of God in our life enables us to live contrary to the culture around us. Many churches have allowed the culture to come in and change them. If the world is at home in a church, that church is no longer a New Testament church.

Can we ask God and expect God to come on us with a new wave of energy and power?

I can only speak for myself. I am willing to take on me the judgment of God. I have not been wantonly rebellious, but on the other side, I have not been all I should have been. I have been careless and lazy. I pray God's judgment on my life to separate me radically from everything that would offend God.

Then I am willing to believe that God will be gracious to me and hear my voice—that He will be willing to multiply my testimony and my spiritual abilities, whatever they are, seven times before the end comes and Jesus returns.

The open invitation is simply this: *Will you join me?* Will you allow the Bible to radically judge your life and separate you from things that are offensive to God in such a way that you will be brought into the manifest presence of God?

Not many will accept this invitation. The Bible speaks of the remnant. I believe that in these last days, only a remnant of believers will accept this kind of an invitation and wholly follow the Lord Jesus Christ.

"Not by might, nor by power, but by my spirit, saith the LORD of hosts" (Zech. 4:6).

## I Surrender All
### Judson W. Van DeVenter (1855–1939)

All to Jesus I surrender,
All to Him I freely give;
I will ever love and trust Him,
In His presence daily live.

All to Jesus I surrender,
Humbly at His feet I bow;
Worldly pleasures all forsaken,
Take me, Jesus, take me now.

All to Jesus I surrender,
Make me, Savior, wholly Thine;
Let me feel the Holy Spirit,
Truly know that Thou art mine.

All to Jesus I surrender,
Lord I give myself to Thee.

Fill me with Thy love and power;
Let Thy blessings fall on me.

All to Jesus I surrender,
Now I feel the sacred flame.
Oh the joy of full salvation!
Glory, glory to His name!

I surrender all,
I surrender all.
All to Thee, my blessed Savior,
I surrender all.

---

Follow Tozer's new writings on Twitter at
http://twitter.com/tozeraw

# Books by A. W. Tozer

## Compiled and Edited by James L. Snyder

*And He Dwelt Among Us*
*The Crucified Life*
*The Dangers of a Shallow Faith*
*Delighting in God*
*A Disruptive Faith*
*Experiencing the Presence of God*
*God's Power for Your Life*
*Living as a Christian*
*My Daily Pursuit*
*Preparing for Jesus' Return*
*The Purpose of Man*
*The Pursuit of God*
*Reclaiming Christianity*
*Voice of a Prophet*

## Books by James L. Snyder

*The Life of A. W. Tozer: In Pursuit of God*
*The Authorized Biography*